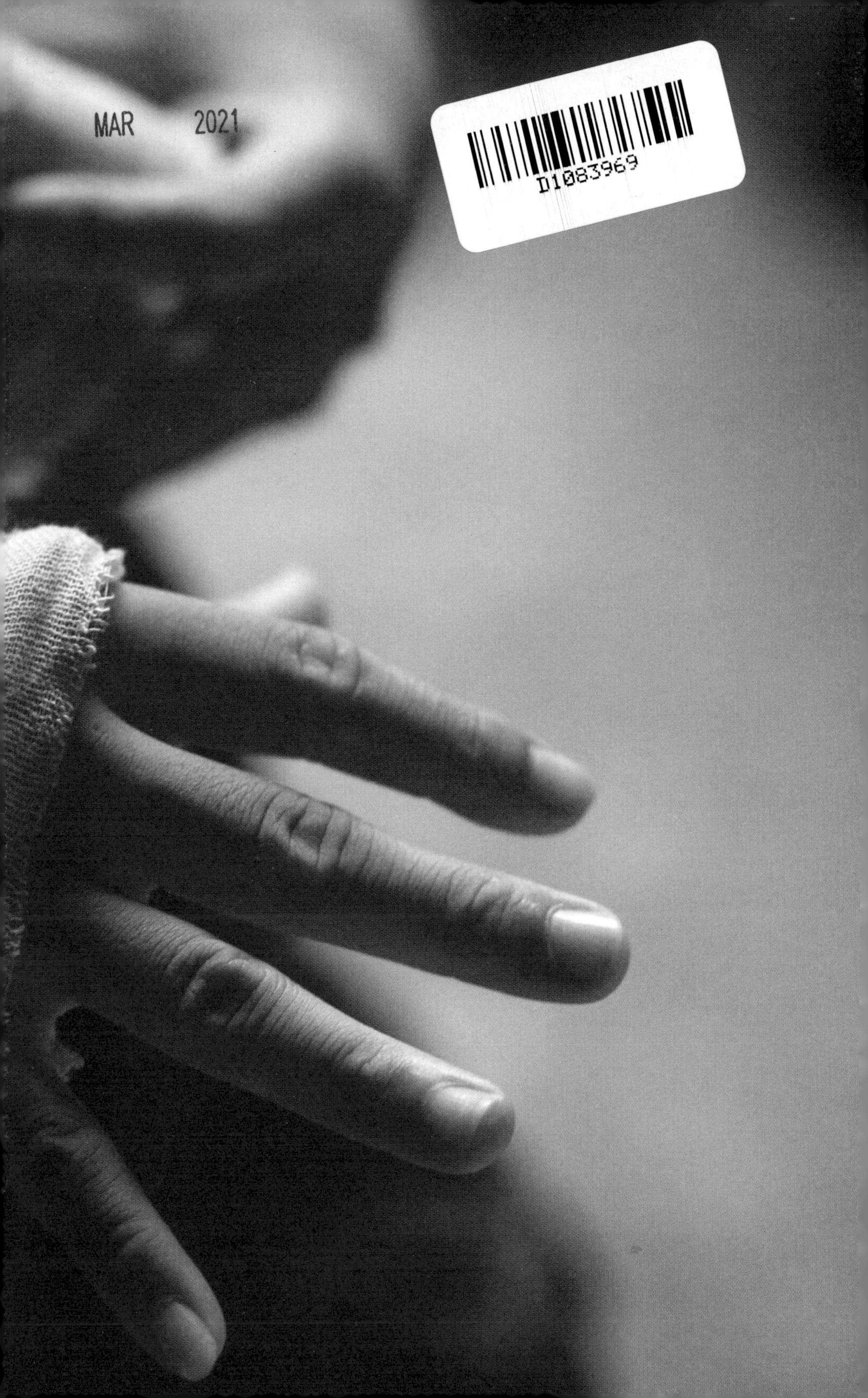

Also available at all good book stores

M A T T   B O Z E A T

FIGHTING BACK

THE **TYSON FURY** STORY

9781785315527

PAUL BANKE AND PAUL ZANON

Staying
Positive

THE STORY OF THE REAL
PAUL BANKE

FOREWORD BY PAUL HAMILTON

9781785315404

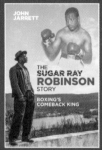

JOHN
JARRETT

THE
**SUGAR RAY
ROBINSON**
STORY

**BOXING'S
COMEBACK KING**

9781785315350

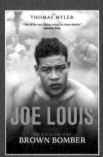

THOMAS MYLER

"One of the best boxing writers in these islands."
Yorkshire Post

JOE LOUIS

The Rise and Fall of the
BROWN BOMBER

9781785315367

TALES FROM
The Top Table

How boxing's superstars
took over a town

CRAIG BIRCH

Foreword by Richie Woodhall

9781785315374

SUPER

THE AUTOBIOGRAPHY OF
SCOTT DIXON

9781785315190

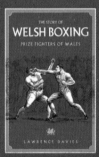

THE STORY OF
WELSH BOXING

PRIZE FIGHTERS OF WALES

LAWRENCE DAVIES

9781785315039

JAMES COOK MBE
MY STORY

GUARDIAN
OF THE STREETS

WITH MELANIE LLOYD

9781785314919

ALEX DALEY

BOXING
NOSTALGIA

★★★★ THE GOOD, THE BAD ★★★★
AND THE WEIRD

9781785314551

amazon.co.uk   **W**
Waterstones   WHSmith

THIS
BOXING
GAME

THIS
BOXING
GAME

A JOURNEY IN BEAUTIFUL BRUTALITY

JOHN WIGHT

First published by Pitch Publishing, 2020

Pitch Publishing
A2 Yeoman Gate
Yeoman Way
Worthing
Sussex
BN13 3QZ
www.pitchpublishing.co.uk
info@pitchpublishing.co.uk

A CIP catalogue record is available for this book
from the British Library.

ISBN 978 1 78531 627 2

Typesetting and origination by Pitch Publishing
Printed and bound in India by Replika Press Pvt. Ltd.

Contents

Dedicated to everyone who's
ever laced up the gloves

*Now, whoever has courage, and
a strong and collected spirit
in his breast, let him come
forward, lace on the gloves and
put up his hands.*

Virgil

*Boxing is the only sport you
can get your brain shook, your
money took and your name in
the undertaker book.*

Joe Frazier

I FIRST met Freddie Roach on a bright sunny morning in a little breakfast place on Hollywood Boulevard.

It was mid-February 1995 on my first day in Los Angeles, having arrived on a transatlantic flight the previous night from London Heathrow. A half-hour drive from the airport along the 405 South and then up to Hollywood via a stop-off at Venice ensured that I was exhausted by the time I booked into the Holiday Inn on Hollywood and Highland, just a short walk from the boulevard. Jet lag rendered sleep impossible and I was up, showered and dressed at six the next morning, before heading up to the top-floor restaurant for breakfast, where I occupied a table by the window. The view comprised an endless expanse of gleaming white architecture, awesome to behold in a part of the world synonymous with movies, fame, celebrity culture, extreme wealth and ostentation, not to mention every kind of weird and wacked-out subculture you could think of. The one thing that Hollywood was most definitely not synonymous with was professional boxing.

I knew very little about Freddie prior to meeting him. Brad, an up-and-coming fighter I knew from back home in Edinburgh, had relocated to LA to train under Roach's tutelage, adamant he was one of the best trainers in the game. At this juncture let me say that boxing was a sport I admired from afar, possessing no more than a cursory knowledge or understanding of its finer aspects. My motivation for coming out here was not to pursue an interest in either the sport or Freddie Roach, but rather to relax and have a good time for a couple of weeks. LA was a city I was already familiar with, having spent a bit of time here a few years previously, and I was looking forward to returning and getting reacquainted with the place.

There was nothing more to it than that.

I'd learned from a mutual friend back home that Brad was living in an apartment somewhere in Hollywood and training at Roach's Outlaw Boxing Gym located on the corner of Hollywood and Highland. My original intention upon arriving was to locate and book into a hotel in and around Venice Beach, the area of LA I was most familiar with, after which at some point I would drive up to Hollywood in the car I'd rented at LAX to check in on Brad and see how he was doing. However, this initial plan changed after I visited two hotels in Venice with a view to booking a room and encountered cockroaches in both. It was around ten at night by the time I'd finished checking out the last of those two hotels in Venice without success. I was dog-tired after a 12-hour flight and therefore decided, fuck it, and got back in the car and drove up to Hollywood, determined to find somewhere decent and clean to spend my first night in the city, no matter what the expense, before looking for a cheaper option in the same vicinity the next day. This is how I ended up at the Holiday Inn just up the street from the Outlaw Gym.

With no idea at what time Brad trained, I thought I would pop into the gym first thing the next morning and find out. I could then either wait for him to appear, or, if he wasn't due until later, kill some time wandering around Hollywood before returning.

So with this in mind I left the hotel for the gym around seven, hoping to find it open or just about to open. It was only a five-minute walk down a Highland Avenue that was already busy with traffic heading in both directions. I soon noticed that the only people out walking were me and a sprinkling of homeless people, carting their belongings with them in plastic bags, or, in some instances, pushing them in front of them in shopping trolleys. The scene was a far cry from the image of Hollywood commonly held around the world. The grim reality of cloying decay and ubiquitous poverty and homelessness came as a shock.

Outlaw Gym took up the entire bottom floor of an office block, surrounded by large tinted windows that enabled you to see inside the place from the street. I reached the pedestrian crossing at the junction opposite and waited to cross. From here I could see that the gym was still closed; there were no lights on and the door was shut. But then, just as I started across the road after the light turned green, the door opened and out came a slightly built guy with cropped red hair and glasses, dressed in an Outlaw Gym t-shirt and training shorts. He proceeded to walk round the corner on to Hollywood Boulevard, then a short distance along before disappearing into a cafe. My instincts told me that this was the Freddie Roach I'd heard so much about.

I decided to follow him into the cafe and find out for sure, intending to find out how Brad was getting on and what time he was due at the gym.

He was sitting at a table in the middle of the place giving his order to the waiter as I walked in. Suddenly conscious of the fact he might not appreciate being disturbed by some guy he'd never set eyes on before while having breakfast, I took a seat at a table by the window rather than approach him right away. The waiter came over, I ordered a coffee, and moments later it arrived. After taking a couple of sips, I made my approach.

'Excuse me, I'm sorry to disturb you. Are you Freddie?' He looked up at me, justifiably taken aback. 'Yeah. How you doing?' he said defensively.

We shook hands as I quickly introduced myself in a manner designed to reassure him that he wasn't dealing with a crackpot, explaining I was a friend of Brad's from Scotland. Noticing him visibly relax, I asked about Brad and how he was progressing.

'Scotty's doing okay [Brad was known as Scotty at Outlaw, due obviously to the fact he was Scottish]. He's working well and looking good. We'll know for sure when he fights in March, though.'

Brad, just so you understand, was a young guy who was in possession of more self-belief than the Red Army on its approach to Berlin. His was the archetypal tale of the bad boy making good, the kind that litters boxing and has done so since time immemorial. After winning the ABA lightweight title – at the time the UK equivalent of the Golden Gloves – he turned pro. A southpaw, he was a slick boxer/puncher with an abundance of charisma, and he was a regular fixture on the back pages of the local and national press, this even though he'd only had six or seven fights as a pro. Filled with the ambition to train with the best, under his own steam he'd made the move Stateside. And so thus here he was, living and training in Hollywood with Freddie Roach.

I quickly warmed to Freddie. He was friendly, open and as real as they come. I would learn that such humility was a rare quality in boxing. At this point he was still some years away from the mammoth success that would see him attain worldwide fame – his picture on the cover of national magazines, being featured in national newspapers, and the subject of TV documentaries – with his services as a trainer in demand by a who's who of the sport's elite fighters. The days of million dollar-plus fees for training Manny Pacquiao were a world away from training the clutch of mainly mid-level guys he was working with when I met him. Freddie was living in two rooms in the back of the gym and was a man of very simple and basic needs. In this respect at least, he never really changed after becoming successful; or at least certainly not in a way you could describe as reflective of that success.

But I'm getting ahead of myself.

During that initial conversation, I recall asking him how he liked living in Hollywood, after he'd asked me how things were in Scotland.

'I don't,' he replied. 'I can't stand cold weather, though. I could never live back in Boston. I used to live in Vegas. I may move back there some day. I only moved out here to work with Mickey.'

Mickey was the actor and movie star Mickey Rourke. Freddie trained him when he decided to give up acting and become a professional fighter, which he did for two or three years. He fought eight times in countries as far afield as Spain and Japan. Rourke had originally been involved in setting up the Outlaw Gym with Freddie, which Freddie subsequently took over with new partners after Rourke decided to move on.

Freddie's friendly persona, combined with a professorial demeanour, was hard to reconcile with a ring career during which he was known as a fighter who never took a backward step, regardless of the opposition. As would become common knowledge, he had Parkinson's. Though he never once voiced regret about acquiring the condition in my presence, he did attribute it to boxing, specifically to fighting past the point when he should have retired. From a fighting family of three siblings, his old man was a martinet who pressured his sons to box or else face hell from an early age. After a solid amateur career in his teens, he turned pro in 1978. His aggressive come-forward style meant that most of his fights were slugfests, responsible for him becoming one of the most popular fighters on the East Coast before moving to Vegas to train under the legendary Eddie Futch, trainer of Joe Frazier among others.

Roach's ring name when fighting was 'The Choir Boy'. His pale Irish skin and flaming red hair meant that he stood out among the Mexicans and Latinos who dominated the lighter divisions at that time. Though he never managed to win a world title, he spent a few years in and around the top ten of the division and in his prime was considered a live contender. He had 53 fights, winning 40 and losing 13. Significantly there are no draws on his record, evidence of the style described. Retiring in 1986, he spent a few years drifting until he discovered a talent for training fighters when Futch took him on as an assistant. In this role, he forged a particularly close relationship with light-heavyweight and former Olympic silver medallist Virgil Hill, who was destined to become his first world champion after he parted company with Futch to train fighters in his own right.

A young guy appeared while we were chatting and joined us. He was one of Freddie's fighters and after being introduced, I decided to take my leave. Freddie told me to come by the gym around 11am, as this was when Brad trained. We shook hands and I left. By now my body was demanding sleep and so from there I headed back to the hotel to get my head down.

Arriving at Outlaw a few hours later, I was confronted by a carnival of noise and activity, to the point where it felt like the walls were about to crack with the energy. On your immediate right when you walked in was the ring. Two fighters were in it sparring as if their lives depended on it, which in a way they did given the stiff competition they were up against for the few opportunities to make anything approaching a decent living in this, the cruellest and most unforgiving of sports. Freddie was standing on the ring apron watching the action, issuing the odd instruction in a calm but assertive voice. This wasn't the time to approach him, so instead I turned my attention to the rest of the place, taking in the guys who were working out on the heavy bags, speed balls, and floor-to-ceiling balls (referred to in the US as double end bags).

Then, looking over to where three or four fighters were skipping (jumping rope) in front of a large wall mirror, my eyes landed on Brad. He stopped as soon as he spotted me in the mirror and we exchanged a warm greeting, one compatible with two guys from the same city and country meeting on the other side of the world. When I told him I'd spent the previous night at the Holiday Inn up the street, he immediately invited me to stay at his place.

Two hours later he was helping me carry a brand new mattress, purchased from a bed shop not far from the gym, into the elevator and up to his large studio apartment on Sycamore Avenue, a few blocks along Hollywood Boulevard. It was a street lined with palm trees and different-sized apartment blocks. As with the rest of Hollywood, at one time the street had been home to aspiring movie stars, directors, producers and all sorts of other movie people. But this was way back in Hollywood's halcyon days. Now Sycamore Avenue, like the rest of Hollywood, was home to an eclectic community of down-at-heel has-beens, aspiring wannabes, ageing rockers and a liberal sprinkling of crack addicts. At night it was not a place for anyone of a sensitive disposition to be walking the streets – this despite the constant presence of a police chopper overhead scouring the streets below with its massive spotlight. Here you could find almost anything you wanted, be it sex, drugs, religion, despair, and destitution alongside fame and fortune. What you would never expect to find in Hollywood was an entree into the rarefied world of prizefighting.

Looking back, there was no better place to start.

I FIRST climbed into a boxing ring to fight competitively two years before arriving in Hollywood and meeting Freddie Roach. I was 26 at the time and did so having never trained, sparred or received any proper instruction in the sport whatsoever. In past years I'd hit a mate's heavy bag a few times in his garage, and fooled around one day at a local boxing gym, but that was it. In other words, I was as green as they come in the last sport you should ever contemplate participating in competitively without first mastering the fundamentals.

The circumstances under which I found myself in the ring were strange to say the least. It was the summer of 1994 and I was working in Brussels. Out for a stroll with a work colleague one particularly hot evening, we happened upon a fun fair that was stretched across almost the entire length of a large park. The place was crowded and with nothing better to do, we decided to take a look. At the far end of the fair we came to a boxing booth. At one time boxing booths were obligatory attractions at fairgrounds the length and breadth of Britain, though by this point long extinct. With no medical supervision or checks, headguards, mouthpieces or hand wraps involved, it wasn't hard to understand why.

But clearly boxing booths were still a popular attraction in parts of Europe, with this one in Brussels the first I'd ever encountered.

So there I was, standing in the middle of the crowd watching a guy on a makeshift stage with a microphone in his hand. Behind him a line of fighters of all shapes and sizes were formed up, complete with the flat noses, cauliflower ears and scar tissue associated with years of taking punches. They were ready for action in shorts and vests and with their hands wrapped, staring impassively at the crowd that was gathered in front of them.

The guy with the mic was addressing the crowd in French, a language I neither spoke nor understood. But it didn't matter. You didn't need to understand the lingo to realise he was challenging the men to step up and take on one of the fighters. Without thinking about it, and on the back of a rush of blood to the head, my hand shot up. The crowd seemed to turn as one in my direction when the guy on the platform pointed me out. He then invited me to pick my opponent from the fighters lined up behind him. My eyes ran along the line and stopped at the guy who was standing on the extreme right. He looked around my height, though leaner and lighter and not as fierce as the others. I pointed at him.

Moments later a guy appeared from nowhere and invited me up to the platform. From up there the crowd looked significantly bigger than it had felt while standing among it. Introductions over, I was led through a curtain into a corrugated iron shed, where thick ropes had been set up in a square to demarcate a ring. It was dingy and stank of damp and stale sweat. It was here in this place that I was about to find out if I was the same man after the accident as before.

This for me, you see, was about more than just experiencing what it was like to go *mano a mano* in a boxing ring. It was motivated far more by the desire to prove something to myself after going through a broken neck some 18 months before. Though by now the bones had healed, the psychological wounds had not. The façade I'd presented to the world after being declared fit after a long period of convalescence was at odds with how I truly felt inside, which in truth was weak and vulnerable. Consequently, subjecting myself to this test was as important as anything I had ever done or would ever do. I knew it from the very second I happened upon the place.

Within minutes the space around the makeshift ring was filled with spectators, each paying the equivalent of a couple of quid for the privilege. My legs were shaking and I was swimming in a sea of adrenalin. I was asked if I wanted to spar or fight for real by the guy who'd invited me up to the platform. A victim of pride, I told him I wanted to fight for real. At this, he instructed me to remove my shirt. Though not a boxer, I had a weight-trained physique, which I hoped and expected would stand me in good stead. I was about to learn otherwise. Muscles count for nothing in the ring unless accompanied by skill. This was to be my first and perhaps most important lesson in the noble art.

The guy placed an old and worn pair of boxing gloves over my hands. Keith, my work colleague, was standing beside me throughout. He didn't have to say anything; the expression on his face from the second I thrust my hand up in the crowd said it all. He thought I'd lost my mind. It didn't matter. He wouldn't have understood even if I'd taken the time to explain. Sometimes insanity is all a man has left. As I was getting ready, my opponent was across the other side of the ring shadowboxing, throwing combinations with impressive speed and the kind of technique and rhythm that takes years to attain. Watching, any confidence I may have retained disappeared like water down a drain. I was about to pay a high price for daring to point him out.

Through the ropes and into the ring we climbed, where the referee (if you could call him that) brought me and my opponent together in the centre. He jabbered a few words in French, spitting them out like a man with something bitter-tasting in his mouth. I was hardly listening. It was the point of no return and by now I couldn't hear or see anything apart from my opponent, standing mere inches away studying me with a knowing grin. He'd been here countless times and could no doubt smell fear. I was a complete novice and he knew it.

We boxed three rounds and I've never experienced chaos like it. The combination of fear and adrenalin drained me of energy and strength within half a round. From that moment it was all about trying to survive, though how to do that when leather is coming your way in rapid-fire sequence, I had no idea. One thing you learn quickly is that the anticipation of being punched is worse than the reality. After receiving two or three, it ceases to hurt as much as you think it will. The biggest shock is just how much boxing takes out of you. Your cardio is sent through the roof – and this after just one two-minute round. The fitness required to go the full 12 three-minute rounds of professional boxing must be phenomenal, it occurred to me later, though as I was to learn, the ability to relax in the ring counts for a lot in this regard.

Each time my opponent came near me, moving with the grace and rhythm of a trained athlete, I lashed out with a wild one-two in an attempt to keep him at bay. I was lucky if I connected with a handful of punches over the entire three rounds, and most of those he seemed to catch and block effortlessly. Never have I felt so naked and alone, standing there in that makeshift ring being picked apart in front of a crowd of spectators, baying for blood.

Yet even with that said, my euphoria when it was over was near elemental. I mean, we are talking a cocktail of relief and endorphins entwined like lovers in frenzied union. The applause and back-slapping that greeted me as I left the ring I hoped meant that I'd given a better account of myself than I thought. Still, I couldn't shake off the feeling that it was an act of kindness rather than respect. Someone tried to thrust a plate in my hand. With this I was expected to go into the audience inviting people to show their appreciation with money. I waved him away. This wasn't about money, and anyway my heart and head were thumping, emotions were running through me like water, and I just wanted to get out of there.

Walking away, I tasted blood for the first time. It didn't matter. All that mattered was that I was still me.

3

THE HARSH, unforgiving code of the Scottish housing scheme is handed down from generation to generation, and is even more fixed and immutable than the laws of the land. In this environment, fighting is accepted as a fact of life for boys growing up, and is crucial to your identity and status.

My own boyhood memories are largely associated with the fear that dogged near every step as I attempted to avoid the tougher lads who could and did make my life hell. While Saughton Mains and Stenhouse, where I grew up, were not the roughest housing schemes or estates in Edinburgh (this particular honour went to places like Pilton, Muirhouse, Niddrie and Wester Hailes), they were rough enough. My older brother and I would take it in turns to go up to the local shops to get the milk, bread and other essentials required on a near daily basis. I still don't know if my mother ever realised the torture she was inflicting on me when it came my turn and she handed me the money and obligatory shopping list. I could only have been around nine or ten at the time, yet I still recall in technicolor detail the terror that filled my pores as I approached the road separating Saughton Mains from Stenhouse. Each time I crossed that road it was like the crossing of a Rubicon, where not only the shops were located but also the Pringles, the Muchies, the Lambs and Nolans lived – boys whose names were branded on my brain like an incubus. Managing to get to the shops and back without incident was a rare feat. The norm was verbal abuse, accompanied by its physical equivalent in the form of a couple of punches and kicks to help me on my way back down the road. I was never able to fathom why they didn't like me. The fact that they didn't meant that I found myself being challenged to a 'square-go' (fight) on a regular basis.

Though I made it my mission never to back down from a fight, I never went into one expecting to win. My ambition extended to just surviving. I lost count of the number of times I found myself lying on the ground hanging on to an adversary's hair for grim life, knowing that if I relaxed my grip even for a second, I was doomed.

My first conscious steps towards rectifying my lowly status were taken at 14. I'd just lost a square-go against Deek Wilson, considered until then the weakest and worst fighter in the scheme and the butt of everyone's disdain as a result. An argument erupted one summer's night during a game of football and I challenged him, safe in the knowledge that even I could batter him. What I did not expect was Matty

Clark, one of the tougher boys, immediately challenging me to fight him first. This meant a certain doing before even facing Deek Wilson. Suffice to say, I arrived home later battered and bruised after losing both fights back to back. The shame burned as I walked across the field towards home, sent on my way with a chorus of jeers and taunts. I would never live it down. Something had to be done.

The answer came to me in the shape of daily sessions on my dad's Bullworker, followed by as many press-ups as I could manage before collapsing on the floor. I didn't have a clue what I was doing but followed this routine religiously night after night over a period of weeks. I would wait until my parents left for their regular session at the pub before going into their bedroom and retrieving the Bullworker from the back of the wardrobe, along with the instructions. For the next 20 minutes or so, I would push and pull the fucking thing in front of the mirror in the living room with every ounce of strength I had. I told no one about my exercise programme; it was a secret. And, anyway, they would all know soon enough when the results started to materialise in the form of a muscled physique and payback to the likes of Matty Clark, Deek Wilson and anyone else who'd ever insulted or derided and bullied me. Just a pity that the Bullworker, and the concept of isometric tension behind it, turned out to be a crock of shit. Weeks of dedicated application, of pushing and pulling and huffing and puffing, at best produced marginal results. Looking in the mirror after six weeks and seeing the same puny body as before, I finally admitted defeat and the Bullworker went back in its box in the back of my dad's wardrobe, where it belonged. I had been, was and would always be a comparative worm in the scheme of things.

But that was before I discovered bodybuilding a year or so down the line, which changed the course of my fate irrevocably. The yearning for respect had not gone away in the intervening period, it had merely dimmed. A chance suggestion by Davie Mackay one day during the school summer holidays resulted in a group of us heading up to a local sports centre. The place in question was designed for the sole use of students attending one of the two colleges that were located adjacent. We sneaked in undetected and spent the next few hours mucking around in the gym. Despite being the weakest when it came to the various exercises we tried, I kept going back. I was determined to get stronger and bigger, and felt instinctively that this was the place to do it. No matter what it took, how long and how much effort was required, I was going to destroy the puny specimen nature had decided was my fate and create the polar opposite – a muscle-bound monster with the strength of a Titan whose very appearance would command respect. Destinies are forged in steel, is a belief I'd imbibed; they are not handed down at birth. I was the embodiment of Nietzsche's *Superman*, turned overnight from just another working-class kid who was destined to spend the next five decades in an unending series of dead-end jobs, into a rugged individualist creating his own path, fuelled by the primacy-of-the-will ethos of the great men in history. I was in tune with the times. It was the early 1980s in Thatcher's Britain, when being working class was no longer something to be proud of but something to escape. My escape was the gym and I scorned those who chose the path of conformity. Where I was from conformity came down to working in a crap job and spending your weekends getting pissed in the local, following the same cycle of despair as your parents and their parents before them. I was determined to go in the opposite direction, to stand apart from and above the herd. I was deluding myself, of course, but in that delusion at this point in my life lay a measure of hope.

By now you may well be asking what any of this has to do with boxing. Well, it's really very simple. At the root of my desire to build a massive body and acquire superhuman strength were the scars of those early boyhood years I'd spent being bullied and disrespected, and my determination to change it. By appearing capable of looking after myself, my intention in building an impressive physique was to deter and avoid ever being challenged. Boxing to the uninitiated is a sport that codifies and glorifies fighting. Its practitioners are a special breed, men who've conquered their fear of fighting – a fear which regardless of the aggressive persona I developed in line with my increasing bulk was still a constant companion. I hated fighting yet admired those who fought. Boxers as a consequence earned my respect on the basis that as big and strong as I was and would ever be, I would always walk in their shadow. The revelation that my insecurities had not been quashed after years of lifting weights in a gym – that instead they had merely been suppressed and concealed – was a hard truth to contemplate.

Thus bodybuilding, in hindsight, was an attempt to take the easy way out. It was evidence of a young man struggling with an ego that had been rendered fragile by an environment in which a distorted conception of masculinity was deified and exalted.

Is it any accident that the majority of boxers hail from the same socio-economic background? In working-class communities in every town and city in every country, fathers take their kids along to the local boxing club to be taught the rudiments of the noble art. Their motive in most cases is not to see their sons develop into world champions – or at least certainly not in the beginning. Instead their motive is to endow them with confidence, self-respect, respect for others, and also, crucially, with the ability to take care of themselves in the street or in the playground in an environment where the role of predator and prey is every bit as central to existence as it is in the Serengeti.

BUT EVEN though boxing today is a sport commonly associated with the working class and deprived communities, it wasn't always the case. History reveals that its original practitioners were typically of the upper classes – the elites in societies in which combat and war were considered noble pursuits (hence 'noble art'), the highest purpose to which men could aspire.

In Homer's epic and poetic account of the Trojan War, the *Iliad*, Mycenaean warriors honoured their fallen comrades with a series of athletic competitions that included an early form of boxing, while boxing was among the games that were held in tribute to Achilles' slain friend Patroclus. Indeed it was in honour of Patroclus that boxing was introduced into the ancient Greek Olympic Games in 688 BC. Fighters trained on heavy bags and wore leather straps over their hands to protect them.

In ancient Rome, meanwhile, boxing was a popular mass spectator sport. And it wasn't only gladiators and slaves who fought for the entertainment of the crowd in Rome, but also free men and even aristocrats. It was just after the fall of the Western Roman Empire when the first attempt to ban the sport was made – in AD 500 to be precise when the then King of Italy, Theodoric the Great, proscribed it on the grounds that it disfigured the face, created he believed in God's image.

But boxing survived, as it did over the centuries all the way up to its modern incarnation, when it was codified with the rules that govern the sport to this day. The man credited with drawing up those rules in 1867 is John Douglas, better known as the Ninth Marquess of Queensberry. However, in truth, the modern rules of boxing were written by a Welshman, John Graham Chambers, with Douglas lending his name to them. But the very fact that a member of the British aristocracy was willing to do so – to endorse this most primitive of sports – should not beguile anyone into believing that boxing was any kind of social leveller during this period. Instead, for Queensberry and his fellow aristocrats, the sport provided welcome opportunities for betting. However, whatever the motives, the advent of the Queensberry rules made boxing more palatable to the public and safer for the fighters. Before the Queensberry rules were rolled out, 'boxing' and 'barbarism' were words that truly did belong in the same sentence.

But even before the rules came to pass which govern boxing to this day, the sport had already experienced growing popularity in England, supported by the rich as a blood sport to rank with any other. King George I, for example, arranged for a ring to be erected in Hyde Park to host a fight involving the country's most famous and popular bareknuckle fighter of his day, John 'Jack' Broughton. Broughton enjoyed the patronage of the Duke of Cumberland at a time when it was customary for members of the aristocracy and nobility to give patronage to specific fighters, financing their training and placing large bets on them whenever they fought.

It was Broughton, in fact, who drew up the first ever set of codified rules of prizefighting. This was in 1743, over a century before the Queensberry rules were established. Broughton's rules stipulated how a round should start and how it should end. They set out the roles of seconds and umpires, and also how the prize money should be divided up at the end. Most significantly, they stipulated that a fight was over when one man couldn't be brought back to the 'scratch line' in the centre of the ring. A few years later, at the instigation of the men who followed and sustained the sport via gambling, boxers were divided into weight categories for the first time – light, middle, and heavyweight – though only one boxer could be the overall champion (for obvious reasons, this was usually the heavyweight).

Broughton went on to establish himself as a promoter too, staging bareknuckle affairs that included what were referred to as Battles Royal, involving the champion taking on multiple challengers at the same time.

The first world title fight – as acknowledged by most boxing historians – took place at Capthall Common in

Sussex on 18 December 1810. It brought Tom Molineux, a former slave from Virginia in the United States who began boxing when he arrived in New York as a freeman at the age of 20, face to face with the English champion Tom Cribb. The stakes involved have been preserved for posterity in the work of the most popular English sportswriter of the period, Pierce Egan, who wrote, 'The pugilistic honour of the country was at stake… the national laurels to be borne away by a foreigner – the mere idea to an English breast was afflicting, and the reality could not be endured – that is should seem, the spectators were ready to exclaim…'

The fight lasted 35 rounds. In the 19th round the crowd rushed into the ring and attacked Molineux, the former slave, who made the mistake of outboxing the English champion. According to accounts, the assault resulted in a broken finger for the American. Regardless, in the open and in the rain, the fight continued and Molineux continued to dominate, until by the start of the 28th round, Cribb appeared out for the count. However, the judicious employment of time-wasting by the Englishman's cornermen, who brought proceedings to a halt on the back of allegations of foul play by the American, allowed him to recover. The Englishman subsequently emerged victorious after Molineux hit his head on one of the corner posts, concussing him to the point where he was forced to concede several rounds later.

Racism was of course key in the ill treatment meted out to Molineux. The former slave alluded to it himself in the open letter he published after his defeat, challenging Cribb to a rematch while 'expressing the confident hope that the circumstances of my being a different colour to that of a people amongst whom I have sought protection will not in any way operate to my prejudice.' The rematch duly took place the following year before a crowd of 15–20,000 people. Tom Cribb again emerged victorious, on this occasion after 11 rounds.

A century later another fighter whose life and career were defined by racism was Jack Johnson.

Born on 31 March 1878 in Galveston, Texas, Johnson was to have a profound impact not only on the sport of boxing but on American society as a whole. Being a black man in the land of the free in the late 19th and early 20th centuries was to be guaranteed a life of menial work and second-, even third-class citizenship. In the South, where the lynching of blacks was a regular occurrence for even the most minor of infractions of a racial code as rigid as it was cruel, it could also mean a death sentence.

Johnson's parents were former slaves – his father Henry of direct African descent – who worked long hours to support their six children. Jack was the second born and the bulk of what little education he received he received at home. School he attended only sporadically until starting work on the docks as a labourer in his early teens. It was here, in the kind of environment where manhood and fighting are one and the same thing, that Johnson was first introduced to prizefighting. Quickly realising that he had a talent for it, he began taking on fellow workers and local hardmen in specially organised match-ups for money from spectators in return for a good fight.

The exact number of fights Johnson had during his career remains a matter of conjecture. Boxing was still largely an underground sport and illegal in many parts of the country. The least number of fights cited is 77, with other sources stating he fought over 100 times. Considering that boxing bouts in the early part of the 20th century could go on for 30 rounds and more, there is no disputing the immense physical ordeal he must have endured in a career that ended at age 60 in 1938. By this point, having lost seven of his last nine bouts, Johnson was inevitably a shadow of his former self.

Jack Johnson's significance in America's social history is rooted in his unflinching defiance of the racial hierarchy that underpinned the nation's dominant cultural values. Blacks, under those values, were expected to know their place. In Jack Johnson, though, this racial hierarchy bumped up against a proud and defiant black man who refused to accept that place. He openly cavorted with white women, dressed like a dandy, and was the epitome of flamboyance outside the ring. In many respects, he foreshadowed the arrival on the scene decades later of another brash young black heavyweight, Muhammad Ali, who likewise was destined to have a considerable social and cultural impact and who cited Jack Johnson as an early inspiration.

After spending years being denied the opportunity to fight for the heavyweight title for no other reason than the colour of his skin, Johnson's chance finally came against the champion Tommy Burns in 1908. Burns, from Canada, took the title after it was vacated by James Jeffries when he retired undefeated in 1905 and who, while champion, had continually spurned Johnson's attempts to challenge him in the ring. Getting Burns to face him was no easy task either. Johnson, in fact, spent two years chasing the Canadian, taunting him in the press and so forth, before the champion finally relented and agreed to face him. The resulting fight took place in Sydney, Australia in front of a hostile crowd of 20,000 spectators.

Even Johnson was unprepared for the wave of racial hatred that was unleashed back home in America in response to his winning the title in a one-sided fight. The heavyweight title was deemed the exclusive property of the white Anglo-Saxon race and meant that the newly crowned champion attracted the venomous hostility of every sector of US society apart from his own. Famed novelist Jack London went so far as to put out a call for a white champion to wrest the title back from the supposed black impostor who was now in possession of it. Thus the era of the 'great white hope' was spawned, a term that was coined by the aforementioned famed novelist.

Johnson was forced to fight a series of white contenders as America's racist boxing establishment set out to find someone to prove the physical and fighting superiority of the white race. Of the series of fights that followed, the champion's encounter with Stanley Ketchel in 1909 was arguably the most memorable. The fight lasted 12 hard rounds until Ketchel connected with a right to the head that succeeded in dropping Johnson to the canvas. As he got back to his feet, Ketchel moved in to finish him off. But before he could unleash another punch he was met with a right hand to the jaw that knocked him spark out. According to legend, the punch was so hard that some of Ketchel's teeth ended up embedded in Johnson's glove.

In 1910 one of the biggest heavyweight fights in the history of the sport took place in Reno, Nevada. Held in an outdoor arena specially built for the event, it was billed as 'the fight of the century' and saw former undefeated champion James Jeffries come out of a six-year retirement to take on Johnson in order to redeem the title on behalf of white America. Such were the times that Jeffries was completely unabashed about the fact, announcing that he felt 'obligated to the sporting public at least to make an effort to reclaim the heavyweight championship for the white race'.

Johnson, though, didn't read the script and proceeded to disappoint both Jeffries and the white establishment when he knocked the former champion down twice on the way to eventual victory in the 15th round. The aftermath saw race riots erupt across the country, in the course of which 23 people were killed. In black communities, there were also celebrations; Johnson's victory deemed so significant that it was commemorated in prayer meetings, in poetry, and forever preserved for posterity in black popular culture.

No matter, dogged by an establishment that was determined to put him in his place, the black heavyweight champion's personal life saw him tried and convicted for violation of the Mann Act, which prohibited the transportation of women across state lines for immoral purposes. Perhaps as a consequence of his being so maligned and rejected by mainstream society, he was a man who sought solace in the company of prostitutes, another much maligned demographic. He was fined and sentenced to prison by an all-white jury, but, defiance running through his veins, instead of meekly accepting his sentence he skipped bail and fled the country to Canada, before heading to France.

For the next seven years he remained outside the US, moving between Europe and South America. He continued to defend his title, though only sporadically, until finally losing it to Jess Willard in Havana, Cuba in 1915. Incredibly, the fight went 26 rounds before Willard KO'd the champion. Returning to the US in 1920, Johnson was arrested and sent to prison to serve out his sentence. It was only in May 2018, after a long campaign, that he was finally awarded a posthumous pardon by Donald Trump.

Jack Johnson was married three times, on each occasion to a white woman. At his funeral in 1948, a reporter asked Irene Pineau, his last wife, what she'd loved about him most. 'I loved him because of his courage,' she replied. 'He faced the world unafraid. There wasn't anybody or anything he feared.'

Other notable figures from the pre-modern period of the sport whose names have endured are John L. Sullivan,

Gentleman Jim Corbett, who defeated Sullivan when they met in 1892, and Bob Fitzsimmons, who in turn defeated Corbett when they fought for the heavyweight title in Carson City, Nevada on St Patrick's Day 1897.

Even the most cursory reading of the lives of those early champions confirms the veracity of the adage that tough times make tough people. Indeed, in hard times a boxing ring is a place to escape 'to' rather than 'from' for young men psychologically battered by poverty and lack of hope. Embracing the ring's life-affirming properties allows those with nothing, or who are deemed to be nothing, to stand tall and proclaim: 'I am.' The ability to do so counts for more than the sport's detractors could ever know.

But more on that later.

THE TYPICAL routine of a fighter consists of roadwork, bag and pad work, conditioning and, most important of all, sparring.

Roadwork usually takes place first in a fighter's daily training routine, often at the crack of dawn when 'normal people' are still in bed. In towns and cities across the world, young and not so young fighters are out running as the sun comes up, or in the dark during the long winter months in those countries cursed to be located in the northern hemisphere. Roadwork to a fighter has long been as fundamental as milk to a baby, the mandatory start to the day in obeisance to a tradition handed down since the sport began.

With that said, though, in recent years new ideas have begun to percolate the sport in conjunction with the emergence and growing influence of sports science, combining the latest knowledge in physiology, nutrition and training techniques. It has resulted in a growing number of fighters questioning the validity and need for early-morning roadwork, based on the damage to joints that pounding concrete day in, day out produces, along with the assertion that roadwork is less efficient when it comes to cardiovascular fitness compared to more modern forms of exercise. No matter, most fighters still consider a form of roadwork integral to their training. Some may opt to do it in the evening to round out the day's training, rather than early in the morning at the beginning. However, do it they must not only for physical but also psychological reasons.

Here it's important to understand that not only must fighters be in top physical condition when stepping into the ring, they must also be ready mentally. This requires that in their training they become acquainted with the experience of going outside their comfort zone, doing so in order to prepare for this very eventuality in the ring. Tough early-morning runs in all weathers, forcing them out of bed at a time when their body would rather still be sleeping, helps to develop the mental strength and fortitude necessary for the ring. And by the way, not all running is equal – certainly not for a boxer. Hills runs, interval sprints, bounding and various other drills come under the rubric of 'sport specific' – in other words, relevant to the ring in the intensity involved and emphasis on engaging the fast twitch muscle fibres used for explosive movements. Long-distance runs at an even pace are about as much use to a fighter as indicators on a submarine.

Prior to arriving in LA and hooking up with Brad at Outlaw, I'd included running in my own training, doing no more than a couple of miles at a time. My pace was never anything but slow and ponderous, symptomatic of my earlier incarnation as a bodybuilder. I still retained a fair amount of bulk on my frame, which ensured that running wasn't the most comfortable experience. Regardless, I considered myself fairly fit just by virtue of the fact I could run two miles without stopping, no matter the pace or intensity.

It was only when I went out running with Brad for the first time that I learned I'd been gravely mistaken. Five minutes from his apartment on Sycamore lay Runyon Canyon Park. Located at the eastern edge of the Santa Monica Mountains, Runyon is an oasis of unspoiled natural beauty slap bang in the middle of Hollywood. A dirt trail as you enter through the gates at the bottom on Fuller Avenue takes you up a steep winding hill for about three-quarters of a mile. Reaching the top, you're afforded a spectacular view of the Hollywood Hills on one side and the entire city stretched out before you as far as the eye can see on the other. You can also get to the top via a more direct and steeper route over rocks and rough ground on the right side of the path as you enter through the gate. Both entail a hike that was challenging enough to qualify as good exercise in itself, yet not so hard that you were unable to enjoy the experience. Thus Runyon, unsurprisingly, was popular with people walking dogs, jogging, hiking – in general those looking to catch some exercise as well as a respite from the madness of the city.

Late afternoons and early evenings the place was packed with an assortment of Hollywood types, who always managed to look as if they'd just stepped out of the pages of a fashion magazine, even while sweating. On any given day you encountered wannabe and established actors, models, movie producers – an entire cross-section of the movie and entertainment industry; their dogs spoiled, manicured and feted like the walking, breathing, barking accessories they were.

Just walking to the top of Runyon Canyon gave you a good workout, given how steep the climb was and the scorching heat of a typical day in LA. Running to the top seemed suicidal to me, yet this is exactly what Brad did four or five days a week as part of his training – and at pace. I say this, of course, after having attempted it myself. At the time I invited myself to run with him, I felt confident I could manage it. It's why I will never forget his words to me as we set off from outside his apartment building.

'You won't make it to the gate.'

We ran to the top of Sycamore, where it met Franklin Avenue, crossing east to west. We turned left along Franklin and ran all the way to Fuller, before making a right on Fuller and hitting the long incline leading up to the entrance to Runyon Canyon Park. I didn't even make it to the gate before collapsing into a coughing and wheezing fit, having to support myself with one hand against the wall adjacent.

'I'll see you back at the apartment,' Brad called to me, just before upping his pace upon entering the park. The temperature must have been in the high seventies and he was wearing a jogging suit with a beanie on his head.

I finally managed to pull myself together, though not before experiencing the ignominy of a couple of passers-by stopping to enquire if I was okay. Thereupon I began a slow trek up into the park and on up the winding path. Finally reaching the summit, I knew I would never be satisfied until I was able to run all the way up there without stopping.

By the time I'd made my way back to the apartment, Brad was already showered and finished his breakfast. His mind was on the gym and his workout in a few hours' time. In the meantime he popped out, while I showered and popped back to bed to lie down for half an hour before joining him at the gym later. I awoke three hours later and didn't make it.

Outlaw Gym was part-torture chamber, part-circus, part-sanctuary and part-rest home for ageing warriors. The variety of characters you came across on a daily basis attested to the mysteries of the human condition. The thing about Freddie Roach, marking him out, was his ability to get along with everybody, no matter what their status or background. Here there was no obvious hierarchy in place according to how important, rich or famous people were on the other side of the door. His business was training professional fighters, one he took immensely seriously, but even so he still made time for everyone, whether it was their first time in the gym or whether they'd been training for years. This told in the atmosphere and energy of the place: serious but friendly, intense but welcoming. The various Hollywood types who were regulars at Outlaw mixed easily with the fighters. That said, the fighters always took priority. One of the first things you learned was the unwritten rule that if you were on a bag or any piece of equipment that a fighter wanted to use, you gave way without hesitation or question.

My initial workouts at Outlaw consisted of a few rounds of shadowboxing in front of a large wall mirror, a few rounds on the heavy bag, the same on the double end bag, and a round on the speed ball to finish. Writing the aforementioned only took seconds; reaching a level of even basic proficiency when it came to working on those pieces of equipment took months and months of consistent practice.

So let's start with shadowboxing.

This is the discipline most fighters use at the beginning of the workout to warm up after jumping rope or skipping, and also invariably end with to cool down. It allows you to loosen up and get your mind ready for work ahead. Beginners and novices typically shadowbox in front of a mirror to check and correct their form, while the more advanced utilise the ring to work on throwing combinations and moving their feet, simulating how they'd move in live sparring or a competitive bout. Watching a top pro shadowboxing is an education in the finer points of the sweet science. The best move with wondrous fluidity and rhythm. To understand what I mean, just watch some footage of a young Ali shadowboxing. It's a thing of beauty.

When it came to my own efforts at shadowboxing, I would throw punches and combinations in the mirror while keeping an eye out for the smirks and knowing looks I fully expected to come my way. I knew without having to be told that my efforts were stamped with the appellation 'novice', absent of any semblance of experience and/or ability. Clumsy, unbalanced, slow, I was all of the above and more. Yet no matter, after just one week in the gym I was addicted to the buzz and atmosphere of the Outlaw Gym and wanted more.

Brad in his training, meanwhile, was looking good, to the point where he consistently drew approving and admiring looks from other fighters in the gym as he worked. Training under Freddie for the best part of six months by now, there was a palpable buzz about him and he carried the aura of a young prospect with bags of potential. It's why everybody connected to the gym was looking forward to his first fight in the States, which was scheduled to take place in a month's time.

The main fighter in Freddie's stable at this point was Justin Fortune, a 5ft 9ins Australian heavyweight. He was an ex-powerlifter and certainly looked like one. His legs were so thick they looked like tree stumps, and he had the arms and shoulders to match. He came to train under Freddie in Hollywood after a spell in London and was 13-1 as a pro (meaning that out of 14 fights he'd won 13 and lost one). Most of his victories had come by way of knockout.

He trained with singular focus and whenever he hit the heavy bag it was always with bad intentions, his punches reverberating like gunshots. He was all business in the gym, aggressive and surly, scowling more than smiling, one of those guys who if he didn't like you made sure that you knew it.

Juan Lazcano, a charismatic Mexican-American lightweight who went by the colourful ring name 'Hispanic Causing Panic', also trained at Outlaw. He'd been fighting as a pro since 1993 after enjoying an extensive amateur career. His biggest fight would come at the very end of his career against Ricky Hatton in Manchester in May 2008. There were many like him at Outlaw – young Mexicans and Latinos for whom boxing was hardwired into their DNA, offering one of the few legal routes out of the poverty whence they came. Every one of them was working and striving to achieve even a fraction of the fame and adulation of the greatest Mexican fighter of them all: Julio Cesar Chavez.

Along with the gym's complement of active pro fighters, Outlaw was also home to its fair share of ex-fighters. Some of them were attempting to become trainers as Freddie had, passing on their knowledge and experience to future prospects or just simply people who were in the gym to keep in shape, while others simply liked to hang out and pass the time reliving old glories. Among them was Troy, a big rambunctious presence who didn't hold back when it came to voicing loudly what was on his mind at any given moment. During his boxing career, he managed to win an intercontinental title, before life got in the way of further progress, as he admitted to me one day. Nonetheless, despite being retired, he still couldn't resist the pull of the ring and sparred on a regular basis, regularly announcing his intention of making a comeback.

Next in line on the invisible totem pole of the Outlaw Gym hierarchy came the fitness people. This was the category I was in and it comprised people of all shapes and sizes, not to mention backgrounds and professions, mostly connected in one way or another to the industry (in Hollywood the film industry is simply referred to as 'the industry'). You had stuntmen, writers, actors, producers and movie executives – individuals who were attracted to the gym's no-nonsense work ethic. For such people Outlaw was an antidote to the rarefied world of Hollywood, where obeisance and supplication are the required currency. Human contact and interaction at Outlaw, in contrast, was stripped bare of all such bullshit. This psychological need for the powerful to feel powerless for a few hours in the week threw up questions about the human psyche which students of Carl Jung would struggle to grapple with.

The gym was also home to a sizeable Russian contingent – made up most prominently of Boris, Alex and Ivan – each of whom you rarely saw smile. They skulked around like men who had bodies stashed in the boots of their cars outside. Boris was an ex-fighter and knew his stuff, while Alex spent more time passing out business cards than training. As for

Ivan, his idea of fun was punching the wall instead of the heavy bag.

I made up my mind to extend my initial two-week stay in Los Angeles to three months. There really was nothing much to go back to and so why not? Being honest, I had to admit that being afforded three months of training at the Outlaw Boxing Gym was as much a reason for staying on as any other. What could I say? At this stage in my life, it was as good a reason as any.

The decision to stay on meant securing the lease on an apartment of my own. This I did in the building directly across the street from Brad's on Sycamore Avenue. The building I moved into wasn't as tightly managed as his, however, with the din of people partying on a near-nightly basis one I had no choice other than to get used to. Things weren't much better during the day – not when the apartment I was renting overlooked the pool and so meant that I also had to put up with the noise of people splashing around. If I'd harboured any desire to try the pool myself, I was instantly cured by the sight of a rat the size of a cat scuttling past it one morning. As you can see, my new accommodation wasn't the best.

After training at Outlaw for a month, along with regular roadwork at Runyon Canyon (though still unable to run all the way to the top without stopping), I sparred for the first time. As anyone who's ever trained in a boxing gym for any amount of time will attest, the ring exerts a pull that becomes impossible to resist over time. No matter how hard and consistently you work on the various bags and other equipment, and no matter how proficient you become, the knowledge that you have yet to take things to the level of testing yourself in the ring against an opponent throwing punches back at you looms ever-larger, until it becomes a monkey on your back challenging you to get in there and face your fears, or else forever walk in ignominy. Nobody asked or invited me to spar, but then nobody had to. The fact that I felt it was enough. It was a dynamic, an irresistible pull which finally prompted me to ask Freddie one morning as I was leaving the gym if I could spar. I asked the question even as every particle of logic and common sense that I possessed was screaming at me not to. But common sense and logic had nothing to do with it; indeed, the very words are antithetical to the primal values of the ring.

Without missing a beat, Freddie called out to a guy who was working one of the heavy bags: 'Hey, Herb, wanna work tomorrow?'

'Sure,' the guy named Herb said, walking over. 'No problem.'

At this, Herb and I exchanged a nod.

'Be here tomorrow at ten-thirty,' Freddie then instructed the two of us, after which I said my goodbyes and stepped out into the stifling heat of a typical LA afternoon.

Herb, I should explain, was a guy around my age who trained every day and had the physique of your average Mr Universe contender: muscular without a trace of body fat. He stood around the same height as me, but there any and all similarity ended. Unlike me, you see, Herb possessed a set of biceps and deltoids the size of cannonballs. He ran half-marathons on a weekly basis and in the gym only Justin hit the bag harder. Though he didn't fight competitively, Herb sparred regularly and knew his way around a boxing ring. Thus, I was doomed. There was no use trying to sugarcoat it; I was destined to be on the receiving end of a public execution the following morning. I could think of nothing else as I took my usual walk back to the apartment along a busy Hollywood Boulevard, dodging in and out of the permanent gaggle of tourists feasting on the Walk of Fame and other attractions, street performers doing their utmost to part them from their money, along with the various other waifs and strays who filled the sidewalk in this part of the world.

The only experience I'd had in the ring before now had come at the boxing booth in Brussels. The crucial difference between then and now was that back then it had come about as a result of a decision made on the spur of the moment, leaving little time to think about what I was doing. On this occasion, on the contrary, I had a full day and night to think about what I was doing.

And what the hell was I doing? I mean, what was I thinking asking Freddie if I could spar?

The more I thought about it the more that dread gripped my insides like a giant pair of gnarled hands. And even though I tried visualising myself in the ring with Herb, jabbing, hooking and moving with studied precision, peppering him with punches as I'd watched the pros do at the gym when they sparred, it was no good. The vision kept reverting to me being punched around the ring at will, struggling to survive a relentless assault from a fitter, stronger and far more skilled and experienced opponent.

I sat staring at the beige empty walls of my tiny studio apartment, complemented by the beige carpet and door, contemplating my fate. Later, I pored over a biography of Muhammad Ali that I'd recently picked up, doing my best to derive inspiration from the story of a man revered around the world as *The Greatest*. I read about his first fight against the feared Sonny Liston in Miami in 1964, when at just 22 he 'shook up the world'. I read too about his epic trilogy of fights with the great Smokin' Joe Frazier and his statement that their last encounter in Manila had been the closest thing to death he'd ever experienced. And what about the *Rumble in the Jungle* in 1974, when he faced a giant wrecking machine in the shape of George Foreman? Going in everyone was sure that Foreman, who was in his prime, would dish out a brutal beating to the former champion. Ali's naysayers going in even included members of his own camp. Yet he prevailed against the odds, utilising his legendary 'rope a dope', which involved him lying against the ropes and allowing Foreman to tee-off on him. In the eighth round, by which point Foreman had all but punched himself out, Ali exploded off the ropes with a lightning combination that put the giant world champion on the canvas for the first time in his career.

What a fighter, what a champion, I remember thinking as I closed the book. Herb, to me now, was every bit as formidable as Foreman was back then. The problem with this comparison was, of course, that I was no Muhammad Ali. In fact I wasn't even one per cent of one per cent of Ali. This realisation only reinforced the dread that just wouldn't let go of my insides.

Given how bad I was feeling about sparring the following morning, you would think the simple thing would have been to pull out, or perhaps fail to show up. Yet it never occurred to me to do either, not even for a second. As bad as things might and likely would get in the ring, they could not compare with the shame of pulling out. No, this was nothing less than a trial of physical, moral and spiritual courage, and there was no question of not seeing it through.

Speaking of which, fear is a word long considered taboo in the cloistered world of boxing, almost as if admitting to it is tantamount to a confession of weakness and/or cowardice. It's no surprise when you consider that the projection of invincibility is and has always been a non-negotiable part of a fighter's emotional and psychological arsenal. The only prominent figure in the sport who ever openly discussed the fear that all fighters struggle with as they prepare to step into the ring was Cus D'Amato, legendary trainer of Floyd Patterson and Mike Tyson. 'The hero and the coward both feel the same thing,' D'Amato, a man who mined the sport to unlock its metaphysical aspects, once mused, 'but the hero uses his fear, projects it on to his opponent, while the coward runs. It's the same thing, fear, but it's what you do with it that matters.'

Much of the pre-fight hype you see in the run-up to a world championship contest consists of exactly that: two fighters trying to project their fear on to one another. In this regard, the master was the aforementioned Muhammad Ali. He was and remains the unrivalled exponent of pre-fight antics, designed to unnerve and shake an opponent's confidence. In his first fight against Sonny Liston, who in his day was every bit as feared by his opponents as a young Mike Tyson was in his, he succeeded in making Liston believe that he was crazy. Whether it affected Liston's performance in the ring is difficult to say, but by convincing Liston that he was unhinged, the man once referred to as the 'Louisville Lip' won the all-important psychological battle before they stepped in the ring.

Expanding on this theme for a moment, the role of psychology in boxing has never been fully explored, which given how important it is in a sport that amounts to unarmed combat is quite astonishing. Yes, many professional boxers are not what you might call conventionally intelligent; as a demographic they are not renowned for possessing a high standard of articulacy, academic attainment, or anything suggestive of time spent immersed in books. Most never attended university or enjoyed anything other than the most basic high school education. Yet when it comes to human psychology, many of them have surely attained a level of proficiency equivalent to a PhD. Ali we've already explored, but what about a young Mike Tyson, who combined boxing skills with an aura of menace yet to be equalled? The plain black shorts, black boots without socks, tight haircut, the way he prowled back and forth in the ring during the pre-fight announcements and introductions, all of it combined to create a sense of dread in his opponents; filling most of them with the belief they had no chance whatsoever and so entered the ring with survival rather than victory in mind. If you don't believe me, go and watch videos of some of Tyson's fights during his heyday in the mid- to late-1980s. The unbridled fear in the eyes of most of his opponents as they stood across the other side of the ring waiting to face him was close to elemental.

The Klitschko brothers, Vitali and Wladimir, are yet another example of fighters who dominated their opponents in advance of their fights. This they would do by dictating the venue, almost always in Germany, the terms of the contracts, and the enforcement of the rules. Thus you would have Vitali representing Wladimir in the changing room of his brother's opponent to supervise his hands being wrapped, as per the rules, and vice versa. This could not have failed to create the impression in the minds of their opponents of being up against both brothers instead of one. It should also be pointed out that the Klitschkos were the exception to the norm in boxing in that they both held doctorates and were academically distinguished, products of the old Soviet system of schools of sporting excellence in which the role of psychology was regarded as paramount.

Floyd Mayweather Jr was a master of psychology and required no doctorate or any other kind of academic qualification to prove it. His particular schtick was and remains the projection of a self-aggrandising, brash, in-your-face persona, wherein he misses no opportunity to boast about his money, cars, houses and liberal spending habits. His ability to get under the skin of his opponents with a ceaseless torrent of braggadocio was near Ali-esque, although on a much more vulgar and unseemly level, it must be said. Prior to the Oscar De La Hoya fight back in May 2007, the undefeated multiple-weight world champion had his opponent rattled on more than one occasion. He did the same to Ricky Hatton during the build-up to their fight later that same year.

It goes without saying, obviously, that all the psychology in the world means nothing without the talent to back it up. Mayweather was a fighter who clearly and most definitely did have the talent. Though his trash talking and antics outside the ring may have given him an edge, when the opening bell went he proved he could more than match it with his preternatural ability. A record of 50-0 as a pro tells its own story (his exhibition bout with Conor McGregor doesn't count in this writer's opinion).

Back to my upcoming sparring session with Herb and the night before I could hardly sleep. I lay in bed running through every possible scenario over and over, trying to be positive but plagued by the nagging truth that tomorrow he was going to use me as a glorified heavy bag.

Even worse than the thought of the physical punishment likely to come my way was the prospect of being humiliated. The ancient Romans called it *dignitas*, the primacy of dignity if a man is to enjoy an honourable and worthwhile existence. My own was under imminent threat of being crushed. The false pride and over-inflated sense of self I'd been endowed with as a consequence of my working-class background was doing its work. It ensured that my dread over meeting Herb in the ring was more to do with the people who would be watching ringside than anything he could dish out. Yet no matter, I was more afraid of being afraid than I was of him. Complicated, I know, but then life is when you're wracked with insecurities, as I was then.

Early the following morning found me shadowboxing in front of the full-length mirrors of the walk-in closet. In just over a month of almost daily workouts at the gym, I'd worked on developing a jab – the punch without which no fighter will go far – a straight right hand, left and right hooks, uppercuts, and on putting them all together in combinations. Doing so standing more or less stationary in front of a mirror in your underpants is one thing. Doing it in the ring against a moving target wearing a pair of 16oz gloves, headgear, mouthpiece, and with your opponent throwing punches back at you, is something else entirely. Even working on the pads/mitts is tough for a novice. The intensity and stress it puts on your heart and lungs is incredible, and by the end of just two rounds in those initial pad workouts, I'd be struggling to get my breath.

My left hook and straight right hand were my weakest shots. In fact they weren't just weak they were fucking horrific, especially the hook. I was having difficulty mastering the concept of pivoting from the hip, thus reducing the left hook in my case to not much more than a weak arm punch. When hitting the pads, you could tell there was no power behind the shot because of the noise it made when connecting – or, to be more accurate, the noise it failed to make. The left hook, in my experience, is the hardest punch to master, requiring as it does the movement of your body from left to right in a short, explosive line that isn't immediately natural. Body mechanics dictate that a left hook should involve bringing your left arm out from your shoulder in order to gain more leverage on it. But in the ring that would be fatal, leaving you open to a right hand while reducing both the power and speed of the punch by disengaging the hips. Indicating to your opponent that you're about to throw a shot by bringing your hand back – 'cocking the shot', as it's referred to – even by an inch prior to letting go is about the worst thing you can do in the ring. Punches must be short, thrown from a dead position with snap and precision. The slightest twitch is a giveaway to an experienced opponent, which is why it takes years to master a craft that from a distance can appear relatively straightforward to the uninitiated.

My right hand was weak due to the trouble I had when it came to transferring my weight from back to front. I was still prone to throwing it as an arm punch – in truth most of my punches were arm punches at this point. A common misconception is that the bigger the arm the more powerful the punch. I could still recall my old man upbraiding me for having skinny arms one summer's day when I was 14, asking me how I expected to punch 'some cunt with arms like matchsticks?' If only I'd had tapes of Tommy 'The Hitman' Hearns to show him. Here was a guy built like a rake but who carried a right hand that was capable of knocking out your average-sized horse.

Punch power is a combination of speed and explosion, the generation of kinetic energy through the body, starting from the back foot pivoting while pressing down hard on the canvas, moving up through the thighs, hips and shoulder, before culminating in the punch. All of the aforementioned muscle groups must be engaged when the punch is thrown to achieve maximum power. When I threw a right hand, they were not.

Yet despite those weaknesses, I continued to try deluding myself that I had enough in the tank to face Herb and hold my own. Okay, he was fit and powerful, also experienced, but so what? He still only had two arms and legs like me. And, yes, he may run half-marathons, but hadn't my own fitness improved since the time I first tried to do the Runyon Canyon run with Brad? I was still unable to complete the entire run without stopping, but by now I only had to stop twice instead of the multiple times I used to back then.

I had a light breakfast, took a few deep breaths to gird my loins, then headed out for the short walk along Hollywood Boulevard to the gym. Another bright and stifling hot day was under way. I passed the usual complement of street performers, people trying to give away audience tickets for TV shows, street artists, tourist guides, tourists and homeless people shuffling up and down with their meagre belongings. It was a street of contrasts and contradictions without the slightest evidence of normality anywhere. It was home.

Reaching the intersection at Hollywood and Highland, the door to the gym stared at me from across the other side of the street. The moment of truth was approaching like a train coming down the track. The light changed and I started to cross. A voice inside was telling me to keep walking. Another was saying, 'You can't back out. You've got to see this through.'

The second voice won out. As if on autopilot, I opened the door and walked into Outlaw. It was 10.15am and my eyes scoured the place, looking for Herb. There was no sign of him and my heart soared with relief. Maybe he wouldn't show up. If so, I was off the hook.

Freddie was standing across the other side of the gym instructing a young prospect on one of the bags. He saw me and waved. I waved back and started getting ready for my workout. As ever, it began with shadowboxing. Over to the right two fighters were in the ring working on the mitts with their respective trainers. One of those trainers was Troy. He saw me, stopped what he was doing and called over, 'Yo, white boy! Herb's gonna knock your ass out!'

He started laughing. I tried to laugh along with him, but my stomach was churning and a weak smile was all that I could muster. I started my second round of shadowboxing and there was still no sign of Herb. Maybe he really wasn't going to show, I thought, starting to relax.

Then he appeared. He had a wide grin on his face and underneath his capped sleeve t-shit his biceps bulged like two small footballs as he shook hands and high-fived people in his usual manner.

'There he is!' Troy's voice boomed from the ring. 'There's the man that's gonna put this white boy to sleep!'

I stopped what I was doing as Herb came over.

'How y'all doin'?' he said, radiating confidence as he shook my hand.

'Good,' I replied. 'How about you?'

'I'm cool,' he said. 'Looking forward to working with you.'

He then walked off to start getting ready, while I returned to the mirror to continue practising throwing combinations. This was going to end badly, I could feel it. The only question was how badly?

Getting ready to spar is akin to going through a solemn ritual associated with a religious order rather than a sport. First you wrap your hands; in this particular instance, my first-ever sparring session, Freddie wrapped mine for me. Fighters use this time to mentally prepare for the ordeal to come. Typically, a look of intense concentration comes over their eyes as carefully and purposefully they wrap – or have wrapped for them – their hands with gauze and tape. A fighter's hands are the tools without which nothing is possible, making them precious and ensuring that wrapping them properly is essential. Vaseline comes next, smeared around the eyes and nose to help avoid unnecessary cuts by moistening the skin and therefore leaving it more elasticised. Some is also placed on the end of each glove to help ensure that when a shot connects, it slides along rather than digs into the skin of your sparring partner or opponent. The cup (groin protector) goes on next, which you step into as if stepping into a pair of trousers. When you put one on for the first time it feels alien and uncomfortable, though not as alien or uncomfortable as the headguard, which leaves you feeling cumbersome. Add to that a pair of 16oz gloves and you feel like a mummy rather than someone who's about to step into the ring to move around and exchange punches with an opponent. The mouthpiece goes in last, which until you become accustomed to it restricts your breathing.

By the time I was ready to walk up the steps to the ring and climb through the ropes, I was already covered in sweat. The combination of the stifling heat that was an ever-present feature of the gym and adrenalin had drained me of energy. Herb arrived in the ring moments later. The entire place seemed to fall silent as we waited for the buzzer to signal the start of the opening round.

Freddie, standing on the ring apron, said to Herb just before we began, 'Remember, he's really green.'

Hearing this, any residue of self-confidence I'd managed to hold on to evaporated. Freddie was trying to protect me, of course, but unintentionally his words had the opposite effect, leaving me bereft of hope that this was going to amount to anything other than abject humiliation.

Each and every time I've sparred over the years, the same feeling has come over me prior to the moment of truth. It's a feeling of calm, an otherworldly calm almost, as the fear, dread and nerves disappear prior to entering a storm. It came over me in Belgium when I fought that guy in the boxing booth, and it came over me now as I stepped forward to face Herb. Everything was reduced to a blur – the gym, everyone watching – as I looked at him and he at me. A strange intimacy enveloped us as we got ready to inflict punishment and pain on one another, creating a bond. No doubt about it, Freud would have had a field day if he'd ever made fighters the subject of his work rather than sex-starved misfits.

The buzzer sounded, we touched gloves, and the action began.

Thud, thud, thud!

Straight away Herb hit me with three jabs, one after the other. He followed with another left jab and a right hand, both detonating off my head. Nothing prepares you for this the first time, nothing, and starting to panic, I put out my left hand in a pathetic attempt at a jab and missed by a mile. Then I tried a right hand, again falling short. Now Herb came forward, hitting me at will. Before long, I was against the ropes being pummelled like a heavy bag.

'Move, get off the ropes! Get your hands up! You gotta move! You're gonna keep getting tagged!'

A plethora of voices were barking instructions at me, but it mattered not; I possessed neither the ability nor the stamina to carry them out. By the middle of the first round it was all I could do to keep my hands up, never mind throw punches. The longest three minutes of my life ended with the sound of the buzzer. I staggered over to Freddie at ringside. He fed me some water. I was so out of breath and the mouthpiece felt like such an encumbrance, I started coughing as soon as it hit the back of my throat.

'You okay?' he asked. I nodded, still coughing. 'Okay, that's enough,' he said. Then, to Herb: 'He's had enough. Let's end it there.'

Freddie undid the headguard and as soon as he took it off, I climbed out of the ring like a man clambering out of hell, conscious of the eyes on me but too exhausted to care. Not even the experience of the boxing booth came close. I wandered over to the chairs and slumped myself down. Slowly, I began to recover; relief vying with humiliation as I played the experience back. One round – one round I lasted. Those who came over to me with words of comfort only succeeded in making it worse. Freddie was in the ring with Herb, putting him through his paces on the pads. Brad was in the far corner working on one of the bags. Justin arrived at the gym just as I started working on one of the other bags, hitting it without much in the way of purpose.

'Hey champ!' Troy's voice rang out. 'You went in the great white hope! You came out the great white dope!'

I got my act together and did three desultory rounds on the bag before calling it quits. As I was packing my stuff away, Freddie came over.

'How you feeling?'

'Like shit.'

'Tougher than it looks, ain't it?'

I forced a smile.

'It gets easier.'

I really don't know why, but I came back for more sparring sessions with Herb after that first one. I also started sparring with Troy, who almost knocked me out with an overhand right during one spar. In time, Freddie's words would prove correct. It did get easier. In fact after a month or so of regular sparring it didn't faze me at all. Where before I felt dread each time I stepped into the ring, now I began to feel excited and couldn't wait to get started. I was able to relax, an essential requirement in boxing, and after six weeks found I could go four and five rounds fairly comfortably. My technique was still shabby, I won't lie, but I was making gradual improvements and crucially my ability to take a shot developed to the point where most of them didn't hurt anything like as much as they did at the beginning. Sparring is actually a buzz. This might be difficult for those who've never sparred to grasp, but it happens to be true. That said, you have to spar consistently in order to maintain the level of mental and physical sharpness that makes it so. Stop even for a few weeks and the old feelings of trepidation return when you climb through those ropes again.

6

WHEN NOT at the gym or training, Brad and I found time to relax. We took in the odd movie at the Mann Chinese Theater, but more often than not we just went for a bite to eat at one of the many eateries that were scattered around the area. We also met up regularly with Ricky, another friend from back home who was living and working in LA at the time. He lived down by Culver City and we'd head down to the Beverly Center shopping mall to meet him for coffee. At the very bottom of Sycamore was located a nightclub that was packed every Friday and Saturday night. The three of us went there a couple of times; Ricky and I safe in the knowledge that Brad's uncommon ability at navigating doormen and club promoters would ensure not only that we got in, but would do so with passes for the VIP lounge.

Sunday was Brad's day off from training and typically we'd head over to Venice and Santa Monica for a day at the beach. Venice Beach Boardwalk was never less than a wonderful glimpse of humanity in all its manic splendour.

People from every part of the world, of every culture and creed, descended to turn it into a carnival of colour, madness and mayhem. I introduced Brad to a deli on the boardwalk where I used to eat regularly back when I first spent time here. They did some great food, cheap too, and so on this particular Sunday we headed there for lunch. The place was busy but we managed to grab two stools by the counter. As we were eating and chatting, a massive bodybuilder appeared, all shoulders and arms in his tiny vest.

He grabbed the vacant stool next to Brad and said with the arrogance of a man for whom size matters: 'Hey li'l bro, slide over.'

To which Brad, with his back to him facing me, replied, 'Ye asking me or telling me?'

The bodybuilder shuffled away.

It wasn't long after this that Brad had his first fight in the States. It was taking place at the Marriott Hotel in Orange County on a bill being headlined by Justin.

If you have never been to Orange County don't worry, you aren't missing a thing. It's suburbia on steroids; the kind of place that gets you thinking that maybe, just maybe, evolution went awry somewhere around Homo erectus. But regardless, it was where Brad was making his ring debut in the States and there was no question of not being there to support him.

As the day of the fight approached, I noticed him become increasingly withdrawn and focused. He was sparring and training well and Freddie was happy with his work. Brad had done well to get in tow with a sponsor back in Scotland who was funding his training and living expenses, which meant all he had to do was train. He'd come to the States looking to develop his career having had a handful of fights at home and winning them all. Prior to this, as mentioned, he'd won the British national amateur title at lightweight, which given that he'd done so straight out of a stretch in prison stood as a considerable achievement. He was a talented southpaw and possessed not just the skills but also the charisma to rise through the ranks in the pro game. This, at least, was the consensus among those who were following his progress.

Still, I couldn't help wondering if he was finding being away from home difficult. He was very close to his family and he also had a girlfriend back in Scotland. I know that he didn't particularly care for Hollywood or LA, but in terms of developing his potential and career in boxing, he couldn't be in a better place or in better hands.

The drive over to Orange County entailed an hour spent navigating a tsunami of traffic on the 405 South. It was an ordeal made bearable by the spectacular early evening sun, hanging low over the horizon like a red spot, casting a majestic hue across the sky as it continued its inexorable descent. Sitting alongside me was Ricky. Though by no means an avid boxing fan, he liked Brad and was keen to support him. The hotel was easy to find off the relevant freeway exit and we pulled into a busy parking lot. A throng of people were milling around by the entrance as we made our way in to collect the tickets that had been left for us at the door.

This was my first experience of a boxing show. The atmosphere at these events is one I would become acquainted with over the ensuing years, and grow to dislike. The combination of the consumption of too much alcohol and the sight of two men trading punches really can bring out the worst in people.

Given the primal nature of the sport, perhaps it's inevitable this is so. It's still ugly to witness close up, regardless.

Freddie and Brad were kind enough to allow me to be present in the changing room to watch them get ready. Just after I arrived, Brad began to warm up. After a couple of minutes of shadowboxing with his gloves on, Freddie began putting him through combination drills on the pads, during which his punches rang out like gunshots – *Pap! Pap! Pap!* His face was a mask of concentration and he looked lean and ready. Watching him, I was sure that not only would he win tonight but that he would do so in style. My confidence only increased when Billy Keane, who was working in Brad's corner as Freddie's assistant, revealed that his original opponent had pulled out. It meant that tonight's opponent was a replacement who'd been drafted in at just one week's notice. This could only be a good thing, surely, I thought.

Justin was sitting quietly by himself on the other side of the room. His fight was the main event and he had an hour or so to wait before he was due to step into the ring.

The tension and adrenalin were palpable and it occurred to me that Brad and Justin's opponents were going through the exact same ritual in another changing room at that very moment. When I left the changing room to return to my seat in the hall, it was with even more respect for fighters than I'd had before.

The place had filled up considerably by the time I rejoined Ricky five rows back from the ring. The din of anticipation immediately erupted into a cheer when the ring announcer climbed into the ring and took to the mic.

'Ladies and gentlemen...'

The daddy of ring announcers is Michael Buffer with his inimitable 'Let's get ready to rumble!' catchphrase. While this guy was no Michael Buffer, he succeeded in getting the crowd worked up to the point where you couldn't hear him because of the noise. Then the fighters for the first bout appeared, making their way to the ring one after the other. Cheers turned to epithets, exhortation and plain abuse as the supporters of each fighter tried to outdo each other in making their voices heard.

I don't remember much of what followed – I was too focused on Brad's upcoming fight to care about much else – but I do recall there were two bouts prior to his, both four-rounders. Four-round fights are for novices and the journeymen that constitute their opposition during this early phase of their career. Thereafter, a novice will progress to fighting over six, eight and ten, until finally fighting the full 12 championship rounds.

Finally, and at last, Brad's fight was next up. The MC announced him and on he came, walking through the crowd towards the ring with Freddie and Billy following behind. The actual fight remains a blur, but Brad lost on points against an opponent he should have defeated comfortably. He seemed to freeze, his movement and punches were stiff and laboured, and he failed to perform. He was a pale imitation of the fighter I'd been watching in the gym over the past few weeks. In the changing room afterwards, the sting of defeat was evident in his demeanour. Months of hard slog in the gym and the expectations whipped up over his potential combined to make the result even more devastating. At Freddie's behest, a promoter had come to the fight with a view to signing him. It was clear without it having to be said that the promoter in question would not now be interested.

Freddie's focus shifted to Justin, whose own fight was now fast approaching. In contrast to Brad, Justin suffered no mishap, making short and brutal work of his opponent with a second-round stoppage. Thereafter the contrast between victory and defeat sat together in the changing room in stark relief; Justin beaming with delight and basking in the compliments being showered upon him, Brad quiet and withdrawn – crushed, you could tell, though putting on a brave face.

An hour or so later, congregated in the hotel room upstairs that had been allocated to Freddie by the promoter, Brad was sitting on a chair facing him, as he sat on the edge of the bed changing his shoes. There was an awkward silence before Brad, to my surprise, spoke up and apologised to Freddie for, in his words, letting him down.

'You know what, Scotty?' Freddie responded. 'I remember I once lost three fights in a row. After the third loss, I said "fuck this" and went on to win the next five. A loss isn't the end of the world. It's about how you come back.'

The drive back to Hollywood from Orange County in the dark was a sombre affair; Brad having decided to travel back with me and Ricky. It was difficult to know what to say so I said nothing, instead allowing him the space to contemplate and reflect on things in the back. To his credit, he wasn't the type to wallow in self-pity. Indeed, quite the opposite, he was extremely hard on himself. He knew he could and should have done better. Anyone who'd watched him train and spar leading up to the fight would have told you that. He was an excellent boxer with fast hands, good power and ring awareness. Freddie spotted his talent the first time he walked in the door of Outlaw. Tonight, for whatever reason or reasons, he'd looked and performed nothing like it.

After dropping Ricky off at his place in Culver City, Brad and I headed up to Hollywood to the Burger King on Highland Avenue, just up from the gym, for a bite to eat. It was late, approaching midnight, and the place was deserted – just a handful of forlorn-looking souls scattered about and a homeless person nursing a cup of coffee before hitting the street for the night. We ordered our food and landed at a table by the window, looking out on to a desolate parking lot. Boxing, I was learning quickly, was no joke. The high of victory was mirrored by the low of defeat with little in between. I felt sorry for Brad as we ate in silence. He was 6,000 miles from home and had spent the past few months away from his friends, family and girlfriend, chasing success in the hardest game there is. The bruises on his face, I had no doubt, were nothing compared to the bruises to his pride. Yet if anyone could recover from a setback such as this, he could. The pride that made defeat so difficult to accept was the pride that would see him come back stronger and more determined.

We finished our food and headed back along to Sycamore Avenue and home. Brad was flying back to Scotland the following day. Outside his apartment building I wished him well and we parted.

I CAN still recall the buzz at Outlaw when the news came through that Justin had been selected to be Lennox Lewis's next opponent. The day in question, I arrived to find him working like a madman on one of the heavy bags. The fight was scheduled to take place in just six weeks' time in Dublin, Ireland, which meant there was no time to waste when it came to getting ready. This was his shot and he knew it, as did Freddie.

The heightened atmosphere was infectious. Justin was a relative unknown with just 14 fights on his record, yet now found himself preparing to step into the ring against one of the most formidable heavyweights in the history of the sport. Lewis vied with the likes of Evander Holyfield and Riddick Bowe for the mantle of the world's top heavyweight. He was a former Olympic champion who at 6ft 5ins tall and anything between 240 and 250lbs dwarfed Justin's 5ft 9ins and 215lbs. It was a classic David and Goliath match-up, one eminently worthy of a Rocky script. Could Justin defy the odds and pull off the upset? This was the question.

It wouldn't be the first time if he did – not when boxing was a sport tailor-made for the romance and emotional pull of the underdog overcoming the odds to achieve the seemingly impossible. The promise of one shot at glory, of crafting a legacy that will live on after you, is the very essence of a life lived fully. And boxing is the one sport that encapsulates this life. Profound, maybe, but never truer than when watching Justin training to face Lewis like a beast under Freddie's guidance; mind, body, soul and spirit totally and completely consumed with the challenge now confronting him.

Like almost everybody else in the gym, I allowed myself to believe that he could actually pull it off and upset the odds. Lewis had lost his heavyweight title the previous year to Oliver McCall and was on the long road back to reclaiming it. Justin had been selected as his next opponent in what his team no doubt considered to be nothing more than a ticking-over fight, keeping ring rust at bay and the former champion busy while his promoter and manager Frank Maloney negotiated the labyrinthine corridors of boxing politics to get him another crack at the title.

Watching Justin work in the days and weeks leading up, as I say, was something to behold. He was not a guy who believed in taking it easy or holding back in sparring, as with some fighters.

As he told me one day: 'There are no friends in the ring.'

I remember watching him spar this young kid who'd just turned pro. This kid's trainer clearly believed that sparring with Justin would help his development. He was wrong. Within two rounds his body had taken such a pounding that it had to be stopped. It was the same story with other sparring partners who were brave enough to share the ring with Justin as the clock ticked down to his date with fate. It reached the stage where Freddie became worried. At this rate they would run out of people to spar with him.

But then, with the fight a mere three weeks away, Freddie managed to secure the services of former heavyweight champ Tony Tubbs to work with Justin. It proved one of the most memorable sparring sessions I've ever witnessed in all my time around the sport, an education in what boxing is all about when stripped back to its purest form.

As mentioned, by now Justin's fight against Lennox Lewis was only three weeks away, which meant he had two weeks of serious training and sparring left prior to fight week – during which it's all about tapering off the training and focusing on rest and recovery. Aggressive and surly at the best of times, now he was like a man getting ready to tear the arse off an elephant. His punches were hard and sharp, leaving Freddie with sore hands every time he worked him on the mitts. Lean muscle covered his body and he was running four or five miles up and down hills every morning.

He was ready.

In contrast, Tony Tubbs turned up with the physique of a man who'd arrived straight from Burger King up the street.

Accompanying him was his wife and his trainer, an old guy who walked with a limp. They were 15 minutes late, time Justin spent pacing around the gym mumbling expletives under his breath, growing angrier by the minute. Tubbs, a wide smile on his face, greeted Freddie with a hug and spent the next few minutes talking to him and various other people in the gym, ignoring Justin in the process. Another 15 or 20 minutes passed before he was ready to step into the ring to start sparring. As he climbed through the ropes, I was certain we were about to witness a public execution.

The buzzer went and immediately Justin moved in and started letting his hands go. Tubbs took every one of his shots on the shoulders and arms, before countering with a couple of short inside uppercuts to back him up. Justin regrouped and came forward again, throwing combinations. This time Tubbs shuffled a couple of quick steps to his left and caught him with a left hook to the head followed by a right uppercut to the body. I couldn't believe what I was seeing. By the middle of the round, Tubbs had Justin against the ropes and was outboxing him. The former heavyweight world champion's skillset was so sublime that he'd succeeded in nullifying Justin's far superior fitness and conditioning.

It took a couple of rounds before Justin adapted to Tubbs's style and began to have success, catching him with some good shots to the body in particular. But this is when Tubbs's experience came into play. Struggling by now with the pace, he began holding and grabbing, tying Justin up in clinches.

He'd gone into survival mode, making it hard for Justin to get off anything clean.

I think they did five rounds before Freddie brought the session to an end. Despite not being able to get Tubbs out of there, as he'd done with most of his sparring partners, Justin would undoubtedly have learned more in those five rounds than in the previous 30 or 40 he'd sparred against lesser opposition. As for Tony Tubbs, he'd just proved that boxing, ultimately, was a sport of skill and will, not biceps and triceps.

My time in LA was now drawing to a close. After three months it was time to wrap things up and head back to Scotland. Even so, I couldn't let things end there. I had to follow Justin's journey all the way to its conclusion, which meant making sure I was in Dublin for his fight against Lennox Lewis. Freddie assured me that he would organise my ticket and gave me the name of the hotel at which he and Justin, along with Billy Keane, would be staying in the city, so as I could hook up with them when I arrived.

With that arranged, I left Outlaw for the last time. The wild and wacky characters I encountered there I would never forget, comforting myself with the thought as I headed for the airport that I would return at some undefined point in the future. During the flight home, I reflected over the previous three months. Regular runs through Runyon Canyon and sparring sessions had left me fitter than I'd ever been. Watching Brad's progress meet with a crushing setback when he lost his fight had given me an insight into the highs and lows that define this sport, while being around Freddie left me with an appreciation of how boxing consumes those who've spent their entire lives doing nothing else.

As for Justin's upcoming fight in Dublin, the enormity of the challenge facing him in the shape of Lennox Lewis seemed more daunting the more I thought about it. Watching him train day in, day out had been a privilege. He had excellent power and under Freddie had worked on getting inside Lewis's long jab to attack the body, spending hours practising bobbing and weaving using a rope stretched across the ring. He'd focused on it in sparring with devastating results against all but one of his sparring partners in the shape of Tony Tubbs. Mentally and physically he was in peak condition. Even so, it was still clear that any chance he had of winning the fight would depend on Lewis underestimating him and coming in under-trained and under-prepared. If he did, if Lewis made the mistake of taking Justin lightly, then who knows, an upset could be on the cards. I wasn't alone in thinking this. Most of the guys at Outlaw were of similar mind. As with most things in life, time would tell.

8

WHEN I got back to Scotland, on a flight I spent sitting next to a man whose stomach, if any bigger, would've had its own postcode, one of the first things I did was book my flight to Dublin along with bed and breakfast accommodation for the weekend of Justin's fight. It turns out I was lucky; U2 were in Dublin the same weekend and accommodation in the city was scarce. At £50 a night I wasn't expecting much by way of luxury, but the place couldn't be worse than some of the places I'd stayed at in my time.

Returning to the grey, cold streets of Edinburgh was a comedown after three months under a blue sky in southern California. Despite the crushing disappointment that hits you in the face when you encounter Hollywood up close, there was something about the place that I'd come to embrace. Every day was different there, unpredictable, while in Edinburgh it was the opposite. Thus I soon found myself itching to leave again, hankering for LA and Outlaw. At least in the short term, I had Justin's fight in Dublin to look forward to. The thought of catching up with him, Freddie, Billy Keane and maybe some of the other regulars at Outlaw who'd be in Dublin for the fight, kept me going.

On a personal level, I was keen to keep up my own training, but I was living in the centre of Edinburgh at the time, didn't own a car and there were no boxing gyms within easy reach. Finally, after a couple of weeks, I decided to bite the bullet and jumped on a bus down to Meadowbank Sports Centre, which housed an amateur boxing club. Walking through the door, I was looking forward to showing off the skills I'd acquired while training and sparring for three months at Outlaw. I changed and headed along the corridor to the sports hall where the boxing gym was based. It was run by one of those old-timers who are the life and soul of the sport, giving of their time to train and nurture young fighters with little by way of recognition or plaudits in return. There must have been around ten or 12 guys there, most younger than me. There was no proper ring. Instead a section of the floor had been squared off with rope, reminding me of the boxing booth I'd fought at in Brussels. The obligatory bags were hanging, scattered around. After a 15-minute warm-up, which involved the trainer putting everyone through a series of floor exercises and drills in a group, I was thrown in with three different opponents, one after the other, each of whom had fought at amateur shows and competitions. We did two-minute rounds, as they do in the amateurs, but it was hard work and I struggled. My sparring partners were younger, faster, fitter and altogether sharper; and by the end there was just no getting away from the fact that I was not put on this earth to box.

I trained two or three times at Meadowbank and never returned, deciding it wasn't worth the hassle of a 20-minute bus journey there and back. I tried one other gym before making my mind up to leave boxing alone. The Outlaw Gym had left too much of a mark for me to be happy with anything less in terms of atmosphere, excitement and the characters I'd rubbed shoulders with. Everything else paled by comparison.

The short flight from Edinburgh touched down at Dublin's Shannon Airport on Friday, 1 July 1995, the day before Justin's fight. The B&B I'd booked was located in a narrow sidestreet a short walk from O'Connell Street, Dublin's main thoroughfare. The city was buzzing and the streets, I noticed, were filled with young people at a time when Ireland's renaissance as an economic hub and cultural attraction was in full swing. I recall reading somewhere that in 1995 more people were moving to Ireland than leaving, marking a departure from a centuries-long tradition. Construction cranes dotted the landscape as the city enjoyed a property boom, while the bars and cafes were packed. It was a time of plenty on the back of the ready supply of cheap money and a sense of perpetual affluence. Writing these words just over two decades later seems surreal, given the extent of the recession that was to impact Ireland and the rest of Europe in 2008. In 1995 austerity and depression were words from a dim and distant past guaranteed never to return.

If only we knew.

As I mentioned, on this particular weekend a U2 gig was taking place in Dublin, which, as the landlord at my B&B wasn't shy in emphasising, meant I was fortunate to have secured the room – a room, he went on to inform me, he could have filled fifty times over. He walked with a limp, his teeth were black and he claimed to be a boxing fan, even though he was unaware that Lennox Lewis was fighting here tomorrow night. This did not bode well for ticket sales, it occurred to me.

As soon as I got to the room I dumped my bag, freshened up and left straightaway for the hotel where Justin and Freddie were staying – the landlord having provided me with directions. Fifteen minutes later I reached the place, approached reception and asked the young woman working there to call Freddie Roach and let him know that I was downstairs. Within minutes he appeared with Billy in tow. In a previous life Billy had boxed as an amateur in Chicago, where he was originally from, before moving to Hollywood to pursue acting. Like most chasing this particular objective in Tinsel Town, he was finding it an uphill struggle and so in between auditions he helped Freddie out, the two of them being close friends. For Billy, even though being over here working in Justin's corner meant missing a couple of auditions, the opportunity of being involved in such a big fight and experiencing Dublin was too good to pass up.

The three of us headed out for a walk. Justin was in his room enjoying his own space, which was completely normal for fighters on the eve of a fight, especially one as massive as this. Most fighters I would come to meet through the years would likewise retreat within themselves just before a fight, as if going through a ritual of spiritual cleansing for the trial to come. For Justin, this was the epitome of a breakthrough fight, akin to a door of opportunity being placed in front of him. Could he pull off the impossible and walk through it into the world of financial security and success that beckoned on the other side, this was the question. Win and, in the inimitable words of Muhammad Ali, he'd shake up the world, propelling himself into the big time. Lose and, well, what did he have to lose really? Nobody apart from his friends and his team thought he had any chance. So, no, a loss to Lewis would not dent Justin's reputation. It was all about how he performed.

Freddie, Billy and I walked along O'Connell Street for a bit, taking in the sights. Freddie was of Boston-Irish stock and therefore possessed something of an affinity with the country, though certainly not to the point where he identified himself as Irish, like many Irish Americans I've come across in my time. Nonetheless, his no-bullshit Bostonian working-class outlook sat comfortably and he seemed very much at ease. I asked him what he thought of Justin's chances over coffee in the small cafe we landed in. I recall him telling me that if Justin could get inside Lewis's jab and find the body, then it would be an interesting night. Justin, Freddie went on, was in better shape than any fighter he'd ever trained coming up to a fight. Working on his head movement and speed over the past few weeks had resulted in significant improvements. He was ready to shock Lewis, whom both Freddie and Billy were convinced would be coming in out of shape, harbouring little if any respect for Justin, given his comparative status as a nonentity in Lewis and his team's eyes. By the end of the exchange, I was convinced that an upset could be on the cards.

We returned to the hotel an hour or so later. Justin was still in his room and Freddie called to see if he was in the mood for company. He invited the three of us to join him and we walked in to find him lying on top of the bed flipping TV channels. It was hard to know what to say, so I didn't say anything. The banter between the three of them was coloured by the kind of choice language you would expect. Justin was a guy who said it as it was, with no airs or embroidery. That's not to say he never laughed or engaged in banter. He did – just not a lot. Usually you found him sporting a scowl and snarling epithets at the startling number of people he didn't like. He was not someone to suffer fools.

'Fuck it, I'm bored with this crap,' he said, referring to the TV. 'Let's get out of here.'

'We've just been out,' Freddie said.

'You stay here then, lazy prick. We'll catch up with you later.'

Grey cloud now hung low over the city skyline and a cool breeze had got up as again I walked the streets of central Dublin in the company of Billy and, this time, Justin. On this occasion we headed off the beaten track, hitting a few sidestreets. I was interested in getting a handle on where Justin was mentally as the fight approached. The psychological aspects of boxing intrigued me more than any other, with legendary trainer Cus D'Amato's injunction on the role of fear in a fighter's psyche the acme of truth.

What is the difference between a hero and a coward? What is the difference between being yellow and being brave? No difference. Only what you do. They both feel the same. They both fear dying and getting hurt. The man who is yellow refuses to face up to what he's got to face. The hero is more disciplined and he fights those feelings off and he does what he has to do.

Implicit within boxing's unwritten but nonetheless rigid code and culture, a fighter must not betray even a hint of fear or doubt coming up to a fight. This does not mean, of course, that they do not experience it. They wouldn't be human if they didn't. But it does mean they are required to control that fear, a feat that involves waging war against natural instincts of survival and self-preservation, and this before even climbing into the ring.

The first time you step into a boxing ring to spar or trade punches, it feels as if you've just stepped into hell. The fear you experience is unlike anything most people could comprehend. It manifests in a surge of adrenalin that drains you of energy. This is further compounded when you start throwing punches and none of them connect. In those first few seconds, you learn that nothing you've done training-wise has prepared you for the reality. Hitting the bag, working on the mitts or pads, does not come close to replicating being in the ring with a live opponent, moving around and trading shots.

For the beginner, taking a punch induces panic. It turns you numb as your inner voice tells you to quit and get out of there. But even stronger are the years of social conditioning you have undergone growing up, making quitting in response to such a physical ordeal tantamount to a disgrace. It means that even in the midst of the hell you're in, you know that bailing out is not an option. It produces an emphasis on survival rather than winning. Forget trying to best your opponent. All you want to do is get through this any way you can. Getting hit repeatedly and remaining in that same space and situation is, on the face of it, the height of insanity. It is why your first ever sparring session ends in an immense and near-overwhelming rush of relief. It carries you along as if on a bed of air and within minutes the ordeal you've just endured is forgotten. In its place comes a sense of pride and satisfaction at having faced your fears and survived.

What makes fighters special is that despite going through that traumatic first experience, they come back for more, buoyed by the belief that the pain, fear and risk is worth it – or at least *will* be worth it in the end. At a certain point they find it gets easier, more comfortable, with repetition. An environment that at first was alien and abnormal starts to feel normal. You know what to expect, you've developed the ability to deal with what to expect, and you begin to relax. Nevertheless, the fear fighters experience before a fight can never be eradicated completely. The difference is that for an experienced fighter, it's more a fear of losing than getting hit or hurt. When it comes to the pros, a loss is more than just a matter of pride. It is also about money and your ability to put food on the table.

When it came to Justin, about to face one of the most devastating heavyweights there'd ever been, a man who stood almost a foot taller, was considerably heavier and had knocked out most of his opponents, the absence of even the slightest hint of trepidation was remarkable. Mentally and psychologically, he was ready for war. Dressed in a loose t-shirt and jeans, he looked about as fit as anyone I'd ever seen up close. I could vouch for the fact he'd put himself through a hellish training schedule over the past six or seven weeks in preparation and his body was rock hard. Still, the memory of that sparring session with Tony Tubbs remained at the forefront of my mind. While fitness and conditioning are non-negotiable factors in a fighter's arsenal, they cannot replace skill nor totally compensate for its lack.

Justin was a skilled fighter, don't get me wrong; he was comfortable with both hands and capable of throwing devastating combinations. But this game is all about levels. It's why Justin going up against Lennon Lewis was like trying to climb Mount Everest in a pair of roller skates.

9

I AWOKE on the morning of the fight nursing a hangover. The previous night Billy and I had made our way over to the Temple Bar district to sample a taste of Dublin's nightlife. We downed a few pints of Guinness and it must have been after 1am when I arrived back at the B&B the worse for wear. Now, after a quick shower, I tentatively made my way downstairs to the dining room to grab some breakfast.

Half an hour later, fed and watered, I was ready to face the world. It had just gone 11am and with time on my hands, I decided to take a wander along to the venue, both to kill some of that time and to make sure I knew where I was going with the fight in mind later that evening. The Point Arena was actually easy to get to. You just had to make your way to the Quayside and from there all the way along by the River Liffey for the best part of a mile. Having said that, I opted to take the small ferry boat rather than walk, feeling more fragile after the previous night's escapades than I thought when setting off.

The ferry had capacity for around ten passengers and I found myself sharing the short journey along the Liffey with a party of American tourists. The temperature had dipped, a chill wind had got up, and the sky hung low and grey. In other words it was a typical summer's day in Dublin town.

The Point Arena looked impressive enough from the outside. I stood there wondering what the crowd would be like later. I hadn't noticed or felt much of a buzz about the fight since arriving. Lennox Lewis, I'd automatically assumed, would be a major draw. But then he was at a stage in his career when many were still unsure what to make of him. Lewis was something of an enigmatic character, capable of producing a spectacular performance in one fight before lapsing into mediocrity the next. After winning the 1988 Olympic gold medal for Canada, he turned pro and relocated to the UK, where he was from originally, to start fighting under the Union Jack. It was a move calculated to endear him to British boxing fans and gain him a fan base. But it hadn't quite worked out the way he and his manager Frank Maloney had planned. The British boxing public had already placed its hopes in Frank Bruno by the time Lewis came on the scene. There was also residual affection for Gary Mason, another prominent British heavyweight at the time. The point is that Lennox Lewis was considered by many British fight fans at this point an interloper, with his decision to box out of Britain as a pro adjudged to be rooted in opportunism rather than the patriotism both he and Maloney had sought to claim. It meant that his only hope of winning over a hard-to-please British boxing public lay in the extent to which he could impress in the ring. He needed the kind of devastating performances that would make him irresistible. As I say, he had already proved capable of doing that with stunning victories against the likes of Donovan 'Razor' Ruddock and the aforementioned Bruno in a scintillating fight at a sold-out Cardiff Arms Park in 1993. Yet those performances had been offset the following year by his defeat to Oliver McCall, an opponent he'd been expected to defeat comfortably. It would take three years before he finally reclaimed the title, with the time in between forming something of an interregnum in his career. Fighting guys like Justin during the intervening period was intended to keep Lewis ticking over and keep ring rust at bay while he waited for his chance to come round again.

After resting up back at the B&B for a few hours, I grabbed a bite to eat at a cheap place nearby then set off once again for the venue. The weather had taken a turn for the better and as I walked along the Quayside, I thought about how Justin must be feeling with only a few hours to go before the biggest night of his boxing career. If he managed to pull off an upset, he was certain of instant fame and promoters clamouring to sign him. If he lost while fighting well and pushing Lewis hard, he could find it difficult to get another big-name fight as he would be considered too much of a risky proposition as a warm-up opponent. It was a cruel dichotomy to contemplate.

The third possibility, of course, was Justin getting knocked out or stopped in the first or second round. If that happened, he would instantly return to the relative obscurity whence he came.

Outside a pub on the other side of the street, the sudden eruption of a punch-up attracted my attention. Two men had just come bursting out of the door of the place swinging. They were both overweight and out of shape, their faces bright red from the effort expended as they threw wild punches back and forth. Behind them emerged a screaming and shouting group of men and women, forming up around them as they continued punching and kicking one another in the street, jeering and cheering them on. The scene transported me back to my upbringing, where fights in and outside the local pub were a regular occurrence.

Boxing at its best is a sport that elevates fighting to an art. It has about as much in common with street fighting and pub brawls as apples have with oranges. Both are fruits, yes, but in terms of taste, touch and appearance altogether different.

I had only just passed the pub and the commotion outside when a silver Mercedes pulled into the kerb just ahead. It contained four men in expensive-looking suits. The back driver's side window came down and a guy thrust his head out.

'Scuse me mate, we're looking for the Point. Is it round here somewhere?'

The accent was unmistakeably London.

'Yes,' I replied. 'I'm going there myself. Why don't you give me a lift and I'll show you?'

'Nice one mate, no problem. Jump in.'

He made space for me in the back and I got into the car beside him. It turned out they were part of Lennox Lewis's entourage and on the short drive to the venue we discussed the upcoming fight. I told them I knew Lennox's opponent, Justin Fortune, and had watched him prepare in LA. Lewis will be making a big mistake if he underestimates him, I asserted. They looked at one another without saying anything to challenge what in hindsight was a bold statement. I'm sure they thought I'd just arrived from another planet. The way I was feeling, I didn't care. I'd grown attached to Justin and Freddie and felt obliged to defend their corner. Spartacus had nothing on me.

We got to the venue and parted with a handshake. Without hanging around, I made my way in. The fight was not going to be a sell-out; this was clear from the thin crowd gathered inside, which came as a surprise and a disappointment. I'd always thought of Ireland as a part of the world where boxing was popular. Was I wrong? But then U2 were playing in Dublin on this night, so who knew?

In the foyer I immediately ran into Tommy Barrett, one of the trainers at Outlaw and an old acquaintance of Freddie's from Boston. He was a straight-talking guy who if he took a dislike to you wasn't shy in letting you know about it. Fortunately I got on with him and it was good to see a familiar face. We went through to the bar and ordered drinks, over which I caught up on the latest news and gossip from LA. There were a few local fights scheduled before the main event and so there was no rush to take our seats. The only fight either of us was interested in was Justin's anyway, and Tommy wasted no time in telling me that if Justin was going to stand any chance he would need a lot of luck along with the performance of his life.

Ten minutes later I left Tommy in the bar and headed into the auditorium proper. The place had filled up in the intervening period, and though still not close to a sell-out the attendance was more respectable than I'd feared it would be on arriving. My seat was six or seven rows back from the ring, in which the last fight on the undercard prior to the main event was drawing to a close. It was an eight-rounder involving a local favourite – at least going by the noise his efforts were generating in the crowd. I watched the last two rounds, which were scrappy, before the local fighter had his hand raised by the referee to a cacophony of cheers and applause.

Now it was time. Justin's shot at causing the boxing upset of the decade was upon us.

'Ladeeez and gentlemen! Here we go! The main event of the eveninggg!'

Butterflies were causing havoc in my stomach as the MC went through the ritual pre-fight announcements. The crowd was strangely muted; certainly nothing like it had been during the previous fight. But, again, Lennox Lewis was just not that popular a heavyweight at the time and Justin was a complete unknown.

'Now, making his way to the ring, from Los Angeles by way of Perth, Australia… Justin Fortunnnne!'

The lights dimmed and suddenly the place echoed to the sound of *Carmina Burana*, one of the most distinctive and powerful pieces of classical music ever written. The spotlight picked out Justin making his way towards the ring. He was in a black robe, hood up with his head down, which lent him an ominous air consistent with the dramatic music he'd selected for his ring walk. Freddie and Billy were walking just behind him on either side. Climbing through the ropes into the ring, he raised his hand to the crowd. Then Freddie helped him out of his robe and he started limbering up with some perfunctory shadowboxing, his thick shoulders and arms glistening under the harsh lights.

'And now, ladies and gentlemen, please welcome to the ring… Lennox Lewisssss!'

Loud reggae music boomed over the PA. Moments later the unmistakeable figure of Lennox Lewis appeared. He had on a white robe and the first thing that struck me was the sheer size of the man. He looked huge compared to Justin and didn't walk as much as swagger in the direction of the ring. He was followed by his legendary trainer Emanuel Steward and the rest of his team. On his face was nonchalance and supreme confidence. He betrayed not the slightest scintilla of doubt or nerves and the crowd couldn't make up its mind whether to cheer or jeer him. When he climbed through the ropes the difference in size between his 6ft 5in and 250lbs compared to Justin's 5ft 9in and 220lbs was simply ridiculous. I'd been keen to see what kind of condition Lewis would turn up in and was delighted when he removed his robe to reveal a body that was on the soft side. It was certainly soft compared to the honed and defined physique Justin was carrying in the opposite corner, evidence of the weeks of torturous training and preparation he'd put himself through. For Lewis, as I said, this was nothing more than a tune-up, a level up from a sparring session and an easy payday while he kicked his heels waiting for the opportunity to win his title back. For Justin, it was the biggest fight of his life, a chance to propel him from obscurity into the big time. The psychological gulf between two fighters facing one another across a boxing ring couldn't have been wider as a consequence. Herein lay Justin's chance. Lewis's poor physical shape relative to Justin's excellent condition filled me with hope, as at that moment I banished the memory of the Tony Tubbs sparring session from my mind.

'Come on, Justin! Come on!'

I was on my feet at the sound of the opening bell as they met in the centre of the ring. Lewis pawed with the jab as Justin immediately started to bob and weave, duplicating the hours he'd spent practising the same under a rope tied across the ring at the Outlaw Gym with Freddie looking on. Lewis, with his signature languid style, long arms hanging loose, was given an early fright when Justin came in low, closed the distance and made contact with a right hook to the body.

'Yesss! Go on!'

Lewis's face registered the effect as he stepped smartly to the side and out of range. Justin kept coming forward, relentless, continuing to move his head to avoid Lewis's long jab as he looked for openings. It was unfathomable but there he was, forcing the former world heavyweight champion to back-pedal; this giant of a man who'd been in with and defeated the best in the business.

The bell sounded at the end of the round amid the cheering of a crowd that had been roused into life by Justin's come-forward, marauding style. To a man and woman they were behind him. My eyes scoured the ringside seats looking for the four suited and booted members of Lewis's entourage who'd given me a lift to the arena. I wanted to see their faces. Disappointingly, they were nowhere to be seen.

The bell rang for the start of the second and Lewis came out throwing his jab rather than merely pawing with it, as he'd done in the previous round. Almost immediately it started to find the target, catching Justin on the way in. Yet Justin kept bowling forward, unleashing a left uppercut to the body followed rapidly by a right to the head. Both failed to find the target as Lewis leaned back out of range before coming back with a double jab. Justin ate them and answered with a jab of his own, causing Lewis to move his head back with a surprised, almost indignant look on his face, as if to say, 'Who the hell do you think you are jabbing me like that?'

The crowd cheered every time Justin came forward. He'd won them over with the sheer audacity and courage of his performance. By the end of the second, he returned to his corner with his chest heaving up and down. The energy he'd expended trying to get inside Lewis's jab had told. Lewis also appeared tired; he was being forced to work harder than either he or his camp had anticipated.

But what Lewis lacked in fitness and conditioning, he made up for with his experience and ring craft. In the third round he started finding his range and soon his punches were having a cumulative effect. By the middle of the round, the much bigger man had asserted his dominance and when the bell went Justin returned to his corner with his face swollen and marked up from the punishment he'd taken. What could Freddie tell him to turn the tables? Since boxing Lewis from the outside wasn't an option, all he could do was continue to try and get inside with the aim of battering his body until his hands came down, then switch to the head. But Lewis had adapted to Justin's tactics and was catching him on the way in.

At the start of the fourth round the crowd roared as if in an attempt to inspire Justin back into the fight.

Alas, it was no good. Lewis now was in command and knew it. His renowned jab was doing its work, snapping Justin's head back time and again, hypnotising him to the point where he was a sitting target, moving neither his head nor his feet. Then it happened. The former heavyweight champ let loose two vicious right uppercuts, one after the other, and both connected, dropping Justin to the canvas. He got up, looking to continue, but instead of the anticipated eight count, the referee waved his arms to signal that the fight was over. A chorus of boos cascaded down from the stands as Lennox Lewis raised his hand in victory, members of his camp joining him in the ring to celebrate. Billy and Freddie, meanwhile, attended to Justin, making sure he was okay, the cutsman dealing with the damage to his face. At one point, Billy turned and saw me in the crowd. He shrugged his shoulders in a gesture of resignation. The fight was clearly stopped early, but even if Justin could've gone on, it was hard to see any other outcome than him taking more punishment. Better to survive to fight another day. He'd acquitted himself with courage and skill, and had certainly surprised Lewis. It was no surprise and all that he deserved when he left the ring to a standing ovation. He could be proud of his performance. I certainly was.

I made my way over to the hotel a couple of hours later. I was due to fly home the following day and was eager to pay my respects and say my goodbyes. I arrived at Justin's room to find them all gathered there chatting, Justin lying on top of the bed with Freddie and Billy sitting in chairs adjacent.

'Hey mate,' Justin greeted. 'How's it going? What do you think?'

His face was marked up but apart from that he looked fine. I stepped forward and shook his hand. 'You were excellent,' I told him. 'You surprised him in there.' I wasn't exaggerating. Justin had indeed given Lewis a surprise, certainly in the first two rounds.

'It shouldn't have been stopped,' he complained. 'That referee's an idiot.'

I asked Freddie what he thought.

'Justin got caught square on with an uppercut. The knockdown was more about him being off balance than the power of the shot.'

There was a knock at the door.

'Who is it?' Justin called.

'It's the promoter,' the voice on the other side came back.

Freddie opened the door to a middle-aged guy carrying a briefcase. 'How's everybody doing?' he said, flouncing into the room with the air of a man who writes the cheques.

Justin looked at him and put his hand out with a knowing smile. And why not? Tonight he'd earned every cent of his purse and more. The promoter (I forget his name now) laid the briefcase down on the side table and proceeded to open it. The business at hand meant it was time for me to skedaddle and so I said my goodbyes, told them I would be back in LA sometime soon, and left.

Five years would elapse before I saw them again.

10

I LOST touch with boxing for a couple of years.

At first, as mentioned, I tried to keep up my training at a couple of local clubs, but it just wasn't the same. What makes an elite gym special, and what makes LA as a town well nigh unique, is that people arrive from all over the world to create a dynamic and an energy that you don't find in small towns and cities like Edinburgh. Everyone there has their own unique story and past, which put together with everybody else's makes for a wonderful mosaic that can't but help energise and motivate. It's a town where you feel you can do and be anything you choose. And regardless of whether it's a sense and a feeling rooted in bullshit, it's still better than walking around pissed off and pessimistic half the time. Living in LA and driving down its wide boulevards under a vast expanse of perfect blue sky is a source of inspiration in itself, lending meaning to the adage that 'the sky's the limit'.

Edinburgh, in contrast, was perennially dreich and grey. I didn't like it and would leave my workouts feeling depressed.

On the way home I would take in the narrow streets, dowdy shops and pale faces of the people and curse the gods for dumping me back. Before long, I stopped boxing altogether and reverted to lifting weights and running as my preferred mode of training and exercise. The Outlaw Gym, Freddie, Justin and all of the guys I'd come to know in my time there, gradually receded from my thoughts as I got on with the business of settling back into life at home.

The only contact I had with boxing during this period was through various books on the sport. I discovered a rich seam of boxing literature going back decades – books on its legendary fighters, trainers and fights, much of it among the best writing I'd ever come across. The biography of Muhammad Ali by David Remnick, *King of the World*, provides a scintillating social history of the US during Ali's formative years in the 1960s. The political and social context Remnick draws leaves you with an incomparable insight into the nature and trajectory of Ali's development as an athlete and political voice of global dimension. His radicalisation growing up during the years of Jim Crow, when blacks living in the South were treated as second-class citizens, suffering under a system of apartheid, makes perfect sense. Ali's years as a devoted follower of Elijah Muhammad and the Nation of Islam, a radical offshoot of Sunni Islam, is both riveting and enlightening. Here was a young man on the edge of greatness after handing a boxing lesson to the feared and hitherto invincible Sonny Liston in Miami in 1964, only to defy the expectations of a white establishment immediately afterwards by announcing his membership of a radical religious and political organisation which held at the centre of its creed the belief that white people were devils.

Sitting ringside at that first Liston fight was Malcolm X, probably the most controversial figure in America at the time. The firestorm that erupted when Ali declared he was a follower of the Nation of Islam was profound, guaranteeing him near-universal opprobrium and the status of pariah overnight. He went from being a precocious, entertaining and charming young boxer with a beaming smile and a cheeky but endearing self-confidence, to someone who posed a threat to the very ethos of the nation's founding ideas. In other words, by refusing to know his place in the tradition of the prominent black athletes and sportsmen who'd gone before (Jack Johnson notwithstanding), Ali was deemed guilty of the heinous crime of setting a 'bad example' to the nation's black population, carrying with it the danger that, inspired by his defiance, they might start getting ideas above their station.

The story of his epic trilogy of fights against Joe Frazier, culminating in the *Thrilla in Manila* in 1975, which Ali described as the closest thing to death he'd ever experienced, is beautifully recounted by Remnick, as is the run-up and aftermath of his historic victory over George Foreman in the *Rumble in the Jungle* in Zaire in 1974, when Ali stunned the world with the first demonstration of his famous rope-a-dope. Remnick also explores Ali's fights against the under-recognised Ken Norton, his contests against the likes of Jerry Quarry, Oscar Bonavena and the enigmatic Floyd Patterson, all of which together mark him out as the greatest heavyweight there's ever been and make him a strong candidate for the title of the greatest fighter there has ever been and ever will be.

Yet Ali's impact as a boxer pales in comparison with his impact on the world stage as a major and totemic political and social symbol. His peak, both as a fighter and figure of defiance, came in the aforementioned 1960s, the most tumultuous decade in America's modern social history. Along with Malcolm X – his mentor and close friend with whom he would split in response to Malcolm's schism with Elijah Muhammad and the Nation of Islam – Martin Luther King, the anti-Vietnam War Movement and the Black Civil Rights Movement, Ali and the 1960s are inextricably linked. It's almost impossible, in fact, to think of anyone else who's lived a more a dramatic and incident-packed life. His sad decline and battle with Parkinson's only succeeds in making what he achieved both in and out of the ring resonate more, proving that despite them, despite him touching greatness, Ali was mortal. In other words, he was not so much a great man as a man who achieved great things.

Another great boxing scribe from the sport's golden age was Budd Schulberg. Schulberg's work is closely associated with a fight venue which more than any other will forever be linked with boxing. I'm speaking, of course, about New York's Madison Square Garden, where ring legends were both born and laid to rest. The crowd at the Garden was considered the most knowledgeable and hard to please of any anywhere. Schulberg, also a reputed novelist and Hollywood screenwriter, captured the drama and excitement of a period in history when gangsters were prominent in and around the sport. Guys like Jake La Motta, active in the 1940s and 1950s, not only battled relentlessly inside the ring but also outside against the US government and the mafia to hang on to their ring earnings. If you wanted to survive in those days, you really did have to be tougher than the next guy.

Scotland's Hugh McIlvanney, for me, occupies a special place in the pantheon of boxing scribes. His ability to say in just one short phrase or sentence what other writers took one or two paragraphs to convey remains unsurpassed. One of his countless classic lines came during his account of Ali's sad demise at the hands of Trevor Berbick in his last fight in 1981: 'To see him [Ali] lose to such a moderate fighter in such a grubby context was like watching a king ride into permanent exile on the back of a garbage truck.'

So what is it about boxing that has fascinated renowned novelists and artists throughout the sport's history? After all, the likes of Jack London, Ernest Hemingway, Budd Schulberg, Norman Mailer, Charles Bukowski, and Joyce Carol Oates have drawn some of their most powerful material and inspiration for their writing from the sweet science. Like no other sport, boxing taps into man's most primitive and primordial reality, stripped bare of the pretence of everyday life with its necessary compromises and emasculating conformity.

Fighters by and large emerge from poverty-stricken backgrounds in the kinds of places where the boxing gym offers both sanctuary and the opportunity of escape from a grim fate. Thus, when you think about boxing the likes of Philadelphia, Detroit, New York, Mexico City and Manila come to mind. In Britain, it's London's East End, Liverpool, Glasgow and Cardiff, places that are synonymous with the mean streets and hard lives that were and remain boxing's bread and butter. On the contrary, my home city of Edinburgh – despite producing one of the greatest lightweights ever to grace the sport in the shape of Ken Buchanan – has by comparison been lulled into a deadening torpor by an overdose of culture and affluence. During the summer months its streets are packed with tourists from every corner of the globe, unable to conceal their excitement at being surrounded by so much history and beauty. Arts festivals, galleries, museums, beautifully kept parks, private schools and grand homes were the things that sprung to mind when you thought about Edinburgh, not boxing. In such an environment the adjectives of combat were as much out of place as beer in a tearoom; as if those primitive attributes of survival – courage, tenacity, ferocity and brute strength – had been diluted to the point of dissipation during centuries in which Enlightenment values of philosophy, science, literature and commerce had held sway.

Yet scratch the surface of its genteel façade and you entered another Edinburgh, one that contained its fair share of working-class and low-income communities – places where the symptoms of poverty were not difficult to find. In such places boxing gyms thrive, offering one of the few legitimate escapes from the truncated lives that are the norm for children of the poor. One such place in Edinburgh was Clovenstone, or Clovie as it was known to the people who lived there. Stuck out on the western fringes of the city, it rose up and fanned across a prodigious chunk of space like a giant monument to concrete and breeze block. It was a part of the Scottish capital where life was lived in expectation of adversity from the cradle to an all-too-often early grave.

In the midst of all this concrete sat the Clovenstone Amateur Boxing Club. More than the church down the road it was here where souls were saved, both from the demons that lurked within and the dangers lurking without. Run by local legend Rab McEwan, this gym is where his son, Craig McEwan, spent his formative years learning a craft that took him to two Commonwealth Games tournaments, representing Scotland as an amateur, and thereafter all the way to Hollywood and Freddie Roach's Wild Card stable.

Two of the most famous amateur gyms in Britain were also located in Edinburgh, across the other side of the city in Leith. Before its gentrification in the 1990s, Leith's claim to existence was the docks that served the ships that once arrived from across the world. Like waterfront communities everywhere, it was the natural habitat of men for whom fighting was as natural as eating. Leith Vic (Victoria) holds the proud distinction of being the oldest amateur boxing club in Scotland, founded in 1919 by a group of local shipyard workers. Sparta Amateur Athletic Club, meanwhile, is where a pre-pubescent Ken Buchanan embarked on his journey to the heights he was destined to achieve, attaining its own distinctive place in the pantheon of venerable Scottish and British gyms as a result.

The wider point worth making is that boxing is an international sport precisely because the hard lives from where it draws its human material transcends borders and cultures. From the barrios of Mexico City to the housing projects of Detroit and the rough housing estates of the East End of London, poverty speaks the same language – and so does boxing. This is the source of its universal appeal. No other individual sport in the world can make the same claim to anything like the same extent.

I RETURNED to Los Angeles in the summer of 2000, five years after Justin's fight against Lennox Lewis on that memorable night in Dublin. In the intervening years I hadn't kept tabs on Justin, Freddie or any of the other guys from my time at Outlaw. Life had moved on. My own training regimen had, as mentioned, fallen into a pattern of weight training combined with regular runs of between three and four miles two or three times a week. I was fairly fit, though nothing like when I was training regularly at Outlaw and running through and up Runyon Canyon when last in LA.

On this occasion I moved back to Sycamore Avenue into a studio apartment in a different building from last time, further up the street. The apartment was clean and contained basic amenities such as a shower, microwave, fridge and hotplate. It was tiny, though – in fact so small you could've been forgiven for expecting the toilet to flush whenever someone pressed the door buzzer by the security gate outside.

Upon settling in one of the first things I did was head along to Hollywood and Highland fully expecting to see Outlaw Gym still there and open for business. I was therefore disappointed to clap eyes on a large FOR RENT sign in the window while approaching the crossing I used to wait at on the opposite corner on Hollywood Boulevard in my previous time here. The memories came flooding back as I crossed over and peered in through one of the large windows. The place was completely bare and empty, inducing a strong if temporary sense of melancholy.

It struck me that Freddie might have returned to Vegas to set up there. I remember him telling me once that he liked Vegas. As for Justin, Billy Keane and the others, who knows where they were now? LA was not a place where people spent a lot of time looking back. People came and went on a daily basis and here there was little room for fixating on the past.

At least Runyon Canyon was the same as I'd left it. Towards the end of my first week back, I ventured out on my old run. It was as tough as it had always been and reaching the top after struggling through the pain barrier more than once, I was ready to collapse. It was early evening, the temperature had cooled, and Runyon was packed. The treat, though, came after I recovered and walked along the short dirt track to the top of the hill from where you were offered a stupendous view of LA, stretching as far as the eye could see. At that moment, it felt good to be back.

It was a couple of weeks later that I tracked down Freddie's whereabouts completely by chance. Deciding to try and locate a gym within easy distance of my new apartment, especially since I did not have transport at this point, in the local phone directory I came across a listing for a place called the Wild Card Boxing Club on Santa Monica and Vine. Before even calling the number to make enquiries, the feeling that I'd just stumbled upon Freddie Roach's new home was inescapable. The name of the place alone gave it away. A quick phone call to the number listed confirmed I was right. After a brief exchange I packed my gym bag and headed over for my first workout, looking forward to seeing Freddie and hopefully some familiar faces again.

Unlike Outlaw, which had taken up the entire ground floor of an office block on the corner of Hollywood and Highland, Wild Card was located above a laundromat in a rundown strip mall that was also home to a strip bar, nail salon and an Alcoholics Anonymous centre. Climbing the stairs from the parking lot in the back to Wild Card for the first time, the familiar sounds of a boxing gym filled my ears – heavy bags being hit with combinations, jump-ropes whipping the floor in rhythmic cadence, voices raised in exhortation, barking instructions and encouragement, and the piercing sound of the buzzer marking the start and end of rounds.

Upon entering, the smell of sweat and leather almost overwhelmed me, as did the heat. The very walls of the place seemed to be sweating, and they were covered with old fight posters and countless pictures of boxers past and present, a common sight in gyms the world over. Immediately to the left, just inside the door, lay the desk. Troy, my old sparring partner from the Outlaw days, was sitting behind it shouting at somebody in the ring across the other side of the gym. Troy, I could tell, didn't recognise me as I approached.

'Hey, how ya doing?' he barked.

'Good. How about you? You remember me?'

'Yeah,' he said, lying. 'How you been? Five bucks if you wanna work out.'

I began digging for the cash when Freddie appeared.

'Hey, how's it going?' he said. 'Good to see you again.'

We shook hands, after which he turned to Troy and told him, 'He's okay.'

That first workout has by and large merged with the multitude that I went on to have at Wild Card over the next five years. I do remember that soon I was blowing out of my arse, lungs struggling for air in the stifling heat. There was no air conditioning and the place was spartan when it came to facilities and equipment. The concept of no frills had been taken to extremes, I remember thinking. In between rounds I recognised a few faces from the past, the Russians, Alex and Boris, among them. Alex, I noticed, was heavier and greyer since I last clapped eyes on him.

'Hey man, where you been?' he said, waltzing over after spotting me across the other side of the gym. 'I haven't seen you in a long time.'

I told him that I'd only just moved back after a few years at home in Scotland.

'Scotland? Why the fuck did you go back there? You'll freeze your ass off.'

I asked him what he was doing with himself these days.

'Still selling cars. Still got my store,' he said. 'How about you?'

When I told him I was writing, the look on his face gave away the fact he wasn't impressed. He said he'd catch up with me later and got on his way.

There were three characters – and I do mean characters – working at Wild Card for Freddie who hadn't been at Outlaw back in the day. Macka Foley, Freddie's principal assistant, was a big ex-pro from Boston. He had the look, countenance and mannerisms of a heavy in a 1950s gangster movie. Now in his mid-fifties, he'd been a journeyman heavyweight between the mid-1970s and early 1980s, taking fights whenever he could to keep him in the party lifestyle he was living then, he told me. His claim to fame was being one of Earnie Shavers' sparring partners during Shavers' prime in the late 1970s. Macka boasted that Shavers used to knock him out once a week. He'd seen action and been wounded in Vietnam as a young man, had navigated the perils of the mob as a debt collector, and fought and sparred with no ambition to do anything other than make enough to get by. As he memorably told me once, 'My life has been a one-man struggle to take it easy.'

Pepper 'Pep' Roach was Freddie's younger brother and properly off his rocker. Like his brother, Pep was an ex-fighter. However, unlike like his brother he went off the rails, fell foul of the law and spent a few years in a federal penitentiary. Upon his release, he began working at the gym. Pep was full of stories from his time in prison, recounted with a liberal sprinkling of colourful jailhouse language, of a kind that would halt proceedings at your average rodeo.

Finally, there was Nigel from the UK – Wolverhampton to be exact. Nigel, or Nige, was a former boxer who'd switched to cage fighting after an eye injury resulted in him being denied a licence to continue to box. At the time in the States, cage fighting was beginning to rival boxing for popularity and participation, largely due to the prevalence of mismatches and a lack of competitive fights that had come to plague boxing – this due to promoters, managers and fighters placing more of a premium on protecting what they had instead of pushing for more, whether it be titles, prize money and/or an undefeated record. Even so, I was never able to take to cage fighting – which later came to be known as MMA (Mixed Martial Arts) – myself. However, returning to Nigel, away from the ring (or cage) he was an affable, friendly personality who was approachable and popular. Billy Keane was still around, though not as much as he'd been at Outlaw. As for Justin, Freddie told me that he'd moved back to Australia running a restaurant. After losing to Lennox Lewis, he lost his next three fights and decided to call it quits. I was surprised to hear it. I really did think he would go on and do well based on his performance in Dublin that night.

So those I've just mentioned were the faces of the Wild Card Boxing Club when I began my time there as a regular in early 2000. They were a rough crew and their voices constantly boomed across the gym as they hectored one another and others without let-up. It soon became a home from home, the people there a surrogate family, always ready with a smile, greeting and the kind of solidarity and camaraderie only those who frequent boxing gyms for any length of time could possibly appreciate.

Over the following few weeks, I settled into a pattern of working on the pads with Pep a couple of times a week. Like Freddie, Pep carried the physical symptoms of too many years spent in the ring. He'd suffered a couple of strokes and while holding the mitts his entire body would shake, even as he urged you to 'hit haarda!'

Speaking of the sport's 'physical symptoms', in every boxing gym you come across them, the casualties of a sport that often takes more than it gives – ex-fighters whose years in the ring will never leave them. In extreme cases it can mean Parkinson's, in less extreme cases slurred speech. Many fighters make the mistake of fighting on past the point of no return when it comes to their health. It's the risk every fighter takes when they lace up the gloves and it's the aspect of the sport that sits least comfortably when judged through the prism of conventional society. This, conventional society, is where human existence is stripped bare of the courage to take risks and reach for something more ennobling than a mortgage, pension and the safe and sure path. Contrast those middle-class values with those of the young men who spend the best years of their lives striving to be the best they can be, enjoying the warm glow of satisfaction that comes with climbing through the ropes and facing their fears. In a very real sense they represent the best of us and as such there's a case to be made that the slurred speech, unsteady gaits and scar tissue you come across regularly in boxing gyms are not the symptoms of physical damage and a deterioration to lament, but rather the physical stamp of a noble spirit.

Moreover, in societies that become ever more unjust and unequal, the boxing gym remains one of the few places where people are judged not on the car they drive, the house they live in, or the size of their bank account. Here the currency of success resides within rather than without. As an old-timer at Wild Card once told me, 'No matter what shit comes my way on the other side of the door, no one can ever take away the fact I had 42 fights. That's 42 times I stood up and said, "I am."'

Among the pros training at Wild Card when I arrived was former heavyweight champion Michael Moorer, whose brooding presence spoke of a man you most certainly would not want to mess with – and nobody ever did. You also had Israel Vasquez, felt by many to be on the cusp of a world title, and Juan Lazcano, who I remembered from Outlaw and whose career had been up and down since. Over the next five years I would come across so many name fighters, contenders, world champions and bona fide ring legends at Wild Card that it's impossible to remember them all, though notable among them were Sugar Shane Mosley, Francois Botha, Virgil Hill, Johnny Tapia and Manny Pacquiao. When it came to the fighter who stood out as the most skilled, outrageous and memorable character I ever saw train at Wild Card, there was no contest. This particular honour went to James 'Lights Out' Toney.

Toney was a veritable force of nature. Whenever he arrived at the gym, the atmosphere underwent an instant and palpable change. He never arrived without an entourage in tow, which always made it seem like an invasion was under way.

'This is ma house!' he would boom from the ring during sparring. 'James mothafuckin "Lights Out" Toney! Who's next?!'

He was merciless in goading and trash-talking his sparring partners, almost to the point where it was public execution and ritual humiliation combined. As far as skills went, watching him at work in the ring, looking back, was a remarkable experience. His movement, ring intelligence and sheer craft took the sport to the level of artistry, belying in the process his street-thug disposition. When he was in shape, Toney's awareness, timing and defence combined to forge a near-perfect package, and even after he ballooned up to heavyweight his skills remained sublime.

He was a master of the shoulder roll and his in-fighting and counterpunching were among the best ever seen in a ring. The way he could find openings in the tightest of spaces when up against the ropes was pure genius, turning a situation that for most fighters left them vulnerable into one that made his opponent vulnerable. As a middleweight in the early to mid-nineties he stormed his way through the ranks, defeating the likes of Michael Nunn and Mike McCallum along the way. Toney moved up to super middleweight and became world champion for a second time after defeating Iran Barkley in 1993. At the time the super middle division was one of the strongest in the sport, boasting a roster of top talent that included the British triumvirate of Nigel Benn, Chris Eubank and Michael Watson. The biggest fight of Toney's career, and one of boxing's classic encounters, took place in 1994 against Roy Jones Jr. Having decided to give up his middleweight belt to challenge Toney for the IBF super middleweight strap, Jones proceeded to outbox him over the distance to win a lopsided unanimous decision. Toney blamed illness and difficulty in making weight for his lacklustre performance that night, testament to the extent to which he was outclassed by Jones.

Whatever the reason, his career went into a tailspin over the next few years. Back-to-back losses followed against a quality of opposition he would have been expected to overcome with little or no difficulty prior to his defeat by Jones. Toney's lifestyle away from the ring was, to put it mildly, chaotic. He went through a very public falling-out with his flamboyant manager Jackie Kallen, resulting in him threatening to shoot her. Thereafter, he nearly disappeared from boxing altogether. But now here he was, back training at Wild Card as a cruiserweight, looking to challenge for another world title.

One Wild Card regular who refused to be intimidated by Toney's antics was Ola Afolabi. This was back around 2002 or 2003, years before Ola emerged as a cruiserweight contender and champion in his own right. Back then he was just another talented kid, perennially broke, who hung around the gym. He liked to laugh and clown around a lot, even when he was supposed to be training, and he never seemed to take anything seriously. He was very likeable and got along with everybody. I remember giving him a lift home on occasion because he didn't have a car and lived miles away from the gym in Highland Park. Normally, he took two buses to get to the gym and home again. Back then he would watch Toney spar at every opportunity. He modelled his own style on Toney's, looking to emulate his defensive and counterpunching skills.

By common consensus, even though he didn't have an amateur pedigree to boast of, Ola Afolabi had the skills but lacked the will to make it in the fight game.

A number of years later, Ola would prove us all wrong.

12

AT NIGHT, Wild Card turned into an unofficial outpost of Eastern Europe with assorted Russians, Armenians and Poles colonising the place. Occasionally, due to my schedule, I would train in the evening. It was on one such evening that I found myself sparring with Ivan. I remembered him from Outlaw back in the day, when he used to train with Alex and Boris. I hadn't seen him since arriving at Wild Card almost a year before – that is, until I ran into him on this particular night.

Ivan hadn't changed much. A large man, he walked around with a permanent scowl and liked to train with his top off. He had big, powerful shoulders, rounded from his years in boxing, and was thickset. His muscles were covered in a layer of fat, ensuring he would not be entering any body beautiful competitions any time soon, and he had the face of a man who'd kissed a few baseball bats in his time. But this was boxing, not bodybuilding, and going by the way he hit the bag, he could certainly bang.

So there I was, happily working away on one of the bags minding my own business, oblivious to my surroundings, when at a certain point I looked up to be confronted by Ivan standing next to me.

'You want to work with me?' he asked in his heavy Russian accent.

I hesitated, and in the short silence that ensued, he sensed weakness.

'Don't worry,' he continued. 'I go easy with you. We just go to the body.'

The inference that I was scared or reluctant to get in the ring with him cut deep.

'No, it's cool, let's do full sparring,' I said, determined to retrieve the situation.

'I can't,' he replied. 'I have a business meeting tomorrow and don't want to get marked up.'

First round to me, I thought, as we walked towards the ring.

With the fact we were just going to the body, there was no need for headgear. I still made sure to use my mouthpiece, though, just in case any of his shots went astray. In the ring anything can and often does happen. By the time the buzzer sounded to signal the start of proceedings, a small audience consisting predominantly of Ivan's buddies had gathered. They were shouting encouragement and instructions to him in Russian. This is when I realised I'd been set up. The bastard had no intention of going easy. He was intent on taking me out.

We met in the centre of the ring. I ventured a couple of jabs to his midsection, both of which he blocked with the cross-arm defence he was using. I next tried a left-right-left hook combination. Again my shots bounced off his arms. He was biding his time, stalking me around the ring, allowing me to burn energy throwing punches while conserving his. Half the round must have elapsed before he suddenly exploded into action with a flurry of uppercuts and hooks. My arms caught most of them, but a couple sneaked through and almost cut me in half.

Any thought of doing anything more than try to survive was now out of the question, as I did my best to keep him off with shots that seemed to land like feather dusters. It was like hitting a brick wall as on he came, boring a hole in my midsection with his eyes. Getting me against the ropes, he again let loose. I took one in the solar plexus and a curtain of pain descended while lurching forward and grabbing on to him. The buzzer sounded and, with it, the onset of a powerful urge to escape through the ropes.

But something stopped me. Quit now and I'd never be able to live with myself, never mind show my face in the gym again. No, fuck it, I had no choice other than to dig deep. There were two rounds left. I had to see this thing through to the end.

Thirty seconds later, the buzzer sounded to signal the start of the second round and off we went. This time I came out more relaxed. I'd felt his power, had taken a shot that nearly downed me and gone now was the fear of taking more. I started throwing combinations and stepping to the side before he could counter. Before long, he was reduced to throwing wild shots that I could see coming and which left him off balance as he missed. By the end of the round, I was on top and feeling pretty comfortable. The third saw him press and put me under pressure. I began to struggle with the pace and grew increasingly ragged. The combination of adrenalin and intensity had drained me and now it was about hanging on. Luckily, he was just as tired and the two of us were reduced to trading slow punches in between clinches that grew longer in duration. It wasn't a pretty sight and when the buzzer finally went, relief surged through me in waves.

Climbing out of the ring, I made a solemn promise never to climb back in again.

I still remember in technicolor detail the first time I set eyes on Manny Pacquiao. It was mid 2001 and I was in the gym training on one of the floor-to-ceiling balls, which were located on the right-hand side of the ring as you came in the door. I was interrupted by a high-pitched voice ringing out above the din. It sounded like someone being murdered. Along with almost everybody else in the place, I stopped what I was doing to locate the source. There he was, this small, skinny Filipino kid shadowboxing in the ring like a pocket tornado. He was wearing a bandana, I recall, and was lightning fast, throwing combinations as if being fired from a pistol. My attention didn't linger, however, as based on his scrawny half-starved physique, I promptly wrote him off, deciding he was likely destined for the same fate of obscurity as the majority of hopefuls who arrived at Wild Card from far-flung regions of the world. Most come from south of the border, hungry to escape the poverty whence they came and to look after hungry mouths left behind. At the gym, Africans rubbed shoulders with Cubans, Puerto Ricans, Mexicans and Filipinos. By far the largest contingent was Mexican. They typically fought in the lower weight divisions and could be relied upon to work like Trojans. They'd upped sticks and relocated to LA with nothing to sustain them apart from a ravenous will to succeed. Freddie, you could tell, respected them, perhaps because they reminded him of his own days as an up-and-coming fighter. Life may have been a struggle in those days, but it was nonetheless simple, uncomplicated and true, imbued with a purpose that most people never experience.

It didn't take long before Manny Pacquiao assumed the unofficial title of main man at Wild Card and top dog within Freddie's stable. Even so, no one could have possibly predicted how far his star would rise. In time I would occasionally find myself running with the large group that accompanied Manny at Griffith Park, putting in some early-morning roadwork. He seemed to thrive on having a lot of people around, evidenced by the large entourage he brought over with him from the Philippines.

Home there was General Santos City, where life is cheap and poverty endemic. The hero status he would come to enjoy in the Philippines called to mind the words of German playwright Bertolt Brecht, 'Unhappy the land that is in need of heroes.' Through the soaring achievements of Manny, Filipinos were able to garner a sense of pride that was otherwise lacking. Indeed, Manny Pacquiao was destined to transcend boxing and assume the status of international icon in the lives of millions not only in the Philippines but all over the world.

It was, I think, 2002 when Justin Fortune pitched up one day at Wild Card completely out of the blue. I was hitting the bag adjacent to the counter when I happened to notice him sitting against the wall watching the sparring that was taking place in the ring. I had to look twice to make sure it was him; he'd put on a lot of weight since the last time I saw him in Dublin back in 1995. In fact he'd ballooned significantly, to the point that when I walked over to say hello I couldn't be 100 per cent sure it was him. Thankfully it was and he stood up and gave me a warm handshake, asking me how I was doing. He'd just moved back to LA from Australia to work with Freddie, he told me. It was good to hear. I liked Justin and seeing him rekindled memories of Outlaw Gym and the drama of his fight against Lennox Lewis. His return to LA to work with Freddie at Wild Card made sense given that Nigel had recently moved on to pastures new. His departure was a source of regret, I have to say, as we'd become good friends. Me and a few of the regulars at Wild Card would descend on his apartment to watch the fights, and he and I also met up now and then for coffee or breakfast. But with his cage-fighting career and profile growing, he'd decided to embark on a full-time career as a personal trainer. His fighting name was UK Hammer and he was eager to achieve something in his chosen sport.

Alas, though, over the next couple of years, Nigel's fortunes would prove that the vicissitudes of life render the idea of making plans absurd. Upon leaving Wild Card, he set himself up at a gym on Beverly Boulevard tailored exclusively to personal training. There he met the guys behind the popular cable TV show at the time, *Jackass*. They filmed a stunt for the show with Nigel and liked him enough to bring him into their circle, where he began rubbing shoulders with celebrities. It led to his services as a trainer being employed by the likes of the filmmaker Guy Ritchie, at the time married to Madonna, and a small part in the Brad Pitt–Angelina Jolie movie *Mr and Mrs Smith*. Now all of a sudden he was making the kind of money he could only have dreamt of when he first arrived in the States ten or 15 years earlier with nothing apart from a dole cheque in his wallet.

For years, Nigel had existed in LA without a car, which was tantamount to heresy in a town where to be without your own transport is to be shorn of status and respect. The paucity of public transport and the sheer size of LA meant that a car was not a luxury but a cast-iron necessity. Now, with his fortunes taking a sharp turn for the better, he was in a position to buy himself a nice four-wheel drive, enabling him to move around and take advantage of the new opportunities that were suddenly opening up. It culminated in Madonna hiring him as her personal trainer on a world tour. His success seemed living proof that the American Dream was both real and attainable, not the myth rooted in bullshit that I had come to believe. All a person needed was tenacity, talent and a shipload of determination.

I lost touch with Nigel soon after that. I'd just moved back to Scotland and my own fortunes had gone in the opposite direction from his. I was therefore shocked when a few months later, I learned from another friend in LA that Nigel had been in a serious car accident and left permanently disabled; said friend going on to reveal that Nigel was confined to his apartment and required round-the-clock care. Initially, I refused to believe it. The thought of someone who personified the words 'fighter's heart' being reduced to such a state was too awful to contemplate. It confirmed to me that in life you don't get what you deserve, you get what you get.

13

SO, YES, Justin was back in the fold, working at Wild Card with Freddie Roach. He was the same assertive, no-nonsense character I remembered. One thing you could never have accused him of was being lazy. He would be up at the crack of dawn each morning to take some of Freddie's fighters out to do roadwork, while in the gym later you'd find him putting them through their paces with workouts designed to develop their power and speed. Then, typically, he would head out again in late afternoon for more roadwork with other fighters. He also initiated strength and conditioning classes at the weekends, which I attended religiously. They were truly torturous sessions and you'd be in pain for a number of days afterwards. It was at one of those classes that I first ran into Andy. We were around the same age and, like me, he boxed to keep in shape. He was big, strong and tough, his gruff Brooklyn accent ensuring that you invariably heard him before you saw him.

He'd been in LA for many years and was pursuing acting, though without much success. We hit it off and became firm friends, drawn together by a shared passion for the gym and a common struggle of maintaining sanity amid the insanity of Hollywood. Andy was also tight with Justin and in the gym the banter was unending. I began to run with Andy and Justin early mornings, either at Griffith Park or up by and around the Hollywood Reservoir, both of which are popular spots with runners in LA.

Nothing compares to early mornings in this part of the world, let me tell you; the cool temperature, blue sky and clean air invigorating and refreshing before the usual smog takes hold as the volume of traffic ramps up. Andy, with his bulk, wasn't a natural runner, but he never stopped trying. Justin, meanwhile, was well on the way to getting back into shape: strong, fit and lean. When we ran there was always an element of competition as we pushed one another to improve. After these early-morning sessions, we'd sometimes head to a breakfast place on Sunset for the customary eggs and coffee. Sitting at an outside table as the sun came up, basking in the reward for the work we'd just put in, life was never better.

Through Andy I also met Nick, a big Croatian guy who'd been here for ten years and ran a health food store on Santa Monica Boulevard. Nick hardly smiled and could have enjoyed a lucrative career playing villains in movies and TV shows, if he'd ever sought one. When I met him, he was sleeping in the back of his store after signing over his other business, a suntan parlour on the corner of La Brea and Sunset, to his wife upon them going their separate ways.

Most days would find the three of us training and sparring together. With Andy sparring was to the body only, which was just as well as he could punch and always went hard. Nick was around my height and a little bigger physique-wise. He preferred to work to the head as well as the body, staying on the back foot and picking you off as you came forward. Though Nick's power was nothing like Andy's, he compensated with better accuracy and timing. Sparring done, we'd usually finish things off with a floor circuit and core work under Justin's supervision, during which we'd be subjected to the kind of verbal abuse you'd associate with being members of a chain gang in the Deep South.

More often than not, after the gym we'd get in our cars and head over to California Chicken on Melrose for a bite to eat. It was a no-frills place, invariably busy, and we'd eat while discussing the sparring session we'd just had, dissecting and analysing our respective strengths and weaknesses like kids comparing toys. The truth was, of course, that as far as boxing went we were slow, ponderous and lacked any real skill. But paraphrasing Brando, it was still nice to kid ourselves that we 'coulda been contenders'.

Around this time a man who really was a contender, James Toney, was getting ready to face Evander Holyfield in what was going to be his first fight at heavyweight. Looking back at old clips of Toney in his pomp at middleweight and super middleweight in the early to mid-1990s, he was now physically unrecognisable from that lithe and lean fighter. He carried a pair of breasts of which any woman would have been proud, along with the waistline to match. Yet, no matter, he still possessed the movement and skills that had already cemented his status as an all-time great. One of the best fights I'd ever seen up to this point was his cruiserweight battle against Vasiliy Jirov, the former Olympic champion from Kazakhstan, in April 2003, a mere six months before he was due to face Holyfield in his first outing at heavyweight. Toney had to dig deep to win a 12-round unanimous decision, dropping Jirov in the last round. It was quite incredible that only a few months later, he was about to make his heavyweight debut against a true heavyweight legend like Holyfield. And though by now nobody would have disputed that Holyfield's best days were behind him, he remained a potent force and was still ranked.

For Toney to be making his debut at heavyweight against Holyfield involved the kind of risk that most fighters would baulk at. The fact he was not a natural heavyweight only made the risk more pronounced. The previously mentioned rolls of fat around his gut as the fight approached were proof that he'd been piling on the weight with scant regard for the kind of weight it was. He was clearly going in believing that his skills and talent would see him prevail regardless of the difference in size and physique. Based on what people knew of Toney's power, it was unlikely we would see a knockout, which meant any chance of him winning would be contingent on his ability to outbox and outfox the former heavyweight champion over the distance. It was hard to square that possibility with the seriously overweight fighter Toney had become. Yet, as I say, in sparring he retained his old elusiveness, slick defence, fast hands and reflexes. Freddie brought in a few big guys to work with him and he schooled them all. I don't think there's ever been a fighter past or present who took a better shot, and in the gym he went round after round without any apparent fitness or stamina issues. I asked Freddie about Toney's chances and he told me that he was confident he could pull it off.

'Holyfield's power won't hurt James,' he said. 'James will take him into the late rounds and he'll run out of gas.'

I wasn't convinced, I have to say. Holyfield was an athlete who turned up in never less than excellent condition. Relatively small for a heavyweight himself, he was still significantly bigger than Toney and his weight consisted of lean muscle. Yes, in terms of skills, Toney was a match for anyone, but for me Holyfield's power would prove the deciding factor. I wasn't the only one who thought that. Justin agreed that Holyfield would have too much power, as did Andy and Nick.

I recall big Macka's analysis of Toney when I asked him about his training methods, which in the gym always consisted of a few rounds of shadowboxing to warm up and then sparring. In fact I can't remember ever seeing James Toney work on the bags or any other piece of equipment. Where he was concerned, it was all about sparring.

'James just needs to get his eye right,' Macka told me. 'His game is all about defence, making the other guy miss and countering. Once he gets his eye right, he's ready.'

Toney certainly appeared confident, shouting and boasting and bragging as per usual in the gym, betraying no hint of trepidation at moving up in weight to face a former world champion and all-round ring legend. His sparring partners were made to work for their money; not only were they on the receiving end of physical punishment but also its verbal equivalent in the shape of dog's abuse. In this respect, Toney was merciless. There was method in his unending tirade of bluster and bravado, though. It was designed, you could tell, to make him appear invincible and indestructible, reflecting the truism that boxing was as much a psychological as physical battle. In adopting such an aggressive badass persona, James Toney was fortifying his courage and confidence while at the same time draining his opponents of theirs.

The fight itself turned out to be a supreme example of skill, defence and all-round ring excellence. Over eight rounds the former middleweight champion boxed beautifully, demonstrating the full repertoire of slick angles, head movement and sublime defence that exemplified his skillset. By the time Toney put Holyfield on the canvas for the first time in the eighth round, the latter had pretty much run out of ideas as well as gas. In the ninth Holyfield's corner finally threw in the towel, bringing to an end what had become a boxing lesson by the smaller man. It was an incredible performance to add to the many that Toney had rolled out during the course of his long career. Due to his brittle and acerbic public persona, perhaps he would never be fully appreciated within the sport. Even more tragic is that as these words are being written, the former world champion and future Hall of Famer cuts an increasingly pathetic figure, deluding himself that he should still be in the ring. He has fought and been humiliated in an MMA contest against Randy Couture and his speech is so badly slurred that it's almost impossible to make out every second word he says.

But then, for the likes of James Toney and Roy Jones Jr, another legend of the ring who many feel went on too long, retirement from the ring was akin to retirement from life itself. And who am I or anybody to advocate a fate such as that for men such as they? On the contrary, when it comes to James Toney, here was a man you would imagine would take up smoking cigarettes if it meant he could fight cancer.

14

ALEX ARTHUR arrived at Wild Card from Scotland to train and spar under Freddie's tutelage towards the end of 2003, just after his defeat to Michael Gomez in one of the all-time classic British domestic fights. I'd followed Alex's career from a distance and watched him emerge as a local celebrity and fighter tipped from a young age to achieve great things. He came up through the amateur ranks, winning almost every tournament in sight, culminating in a gold medal at the 1998 Commonwealth Games in Kuala Lumpur.

Turning pro immediately afterwards, he proceeded to build an unbeaten record and seemed well on the way to a future that would include world titles. He was the golden boy not only of Scottish but British boxing for a while, a status aided by his media-friendly personality and articulacy. For a spell he drew comparisons with Ken Buchanan, who early on endorsed his talent and spoke favourably about his potential. Indeed for a period the world looked to be Alex

Arthur's oyster. That is until he lost to Michael Gomez in his first defeat as a professional.

Freddie told me Alex would be arriving to train and spar for a couple of weeks. He hadn't long taken on the role of Alex's head trainer, despite not being able to make it over to Edinburgh to work his corner for the Gomez fight. In his place had been Alex's long-time coach, Terry McCormack, who in advance of his arrival at Wild Card flew over to sit down with Freddie and plan his training schedule. I'd never met Alex personally and was looking forward to seeing him train and spar.

Along with his brother Mark, who'd travelled with him, Alex planned to stay in LA for three weeks. They were staying with Bernard Dunne, an Irish prospect training at Wild Card under Freddie at the time, at his apartment in Santa Monica. Bernard would go on to win the world super bantamweight title in a classic encounter with Argentina's Ricardo Cordoba in front of his own fans in Dublin in 2009. However, that was still five years down the road. At this stage in his career, Bernard was just another young fighter who'd made the pilgrimage to Hollywood to train at Wild Card, eager to develop his craft and make his way in the sport. He was a popular figure in the gym and already knew Alex from their days in the amateurs.

Freddie, as mentioned, had not been in Alex's corner for the Gomez fight, which was already suggestive of a relationship that wasn't destined to last. It was obvious that Freddie would not be minded to fly halfway across the world to train a fighter for the kind of fee that Alex could offer for his services. This was no reflection on Alex; he was an excellent boxer and a champion in his own right. But he wasn't fighting at the same level as Manny Pacquiao and money, as they say, talks.

I recall giving Alex and his brother a lift from the gym back to Bernard's apartment in Santa Monica one day. I took Santa Monica Boulevard all the way in order to give them a look at Beverly Hills, which we passed through. If Alex was impressed, he wasn't showing it. A working-class lad from a housing estate in Scotland, boxing had provided him with an escape to a better life. Countless years of torturous early-morning roadwork, sparring and training had gone into providing him with a measure of financial security. Traditionally, and sadly, money had bewitched and blinded fighters; young men who typically come from nothing to find themselves in a position to afford the finer things in life, only to wind up spending more than they save and entering retirement broke – or close to it. Alex Arthur, you got the sense, would not fall into the same trap. He just too switched on and focused for that to happen.

During his time at Wild Card, he looked impressive in sparring. Freddie put him in with the likes of Israel Vasquez, Bernard Dunne and former world champion Nate Campbell. Alex handled them all comfortably. Everybody watching was impressed, including Freddie. When I asked him what he thought of Arthur, I recall that he told me, 'Very good. He just needs to let his hands go a bit more.'

In the ring, Alex exuded elegance, poise and craft. Amid the countless gym wars that took place at Wild Card, it was unusual to watch a fighter bring the particular kind of control and intelligence to their work that he did. The biggest compliment he could have received in recognition of his talent came when other fighters in the gym stopped their training to watch him spar. Rather than being fazed by the attention and scrutiny, he appeared to revel in it, inspiring him to perform better.

He climbed out the ring after that first day of sparring glowing with the aura of a fighter who knew he'd done well in front of an audience of contenders, fighters and trainers who knew their stuff. The lift it gave him was exactly what he needed after the Gomez fight, providing further evidence that fighters exist, like precarious economies, between extremes of buoyant surplus and crippling deficit when it comes to that most precious of commodities: confidence.

By the time he left to return to Scotland, Alex Arthur had succeeded in making a favourable impression at Wild Card. However, with that said, Freddie was not destined to be his trainer going forward. He had too many commitments Stateside and with Manny's career moving into overdrive, his priorities were clear. Alex wasn't a stupid guy; he knew it too. Here was a fighter who did not function well as part of a stable, who liked to be in control of every aspect of his career, including who trained him, where and how. Indeed, throughout his career he'd come in for criticism for constantly changing trainers. At one point, though of course a slight exaggeration, it seemed Alex had a different trainer in his corner for every fight. It was the pattern of a fighter who could never find a trainer whose knowledge and judgement he completely trusted. Yet rather than being the weakness some asserted, it may on the contrary have been a strength, reflective of his single-mindedness and assertiveness, which for a boxer are vital attributes. All in all, Alex Arthur was an interesting guy with a fierce sense of self. Our paths were destined to cross again a few years down the line. When they did, these initial impressions I formed of him in LA would remain.

15

AT WILD Card, the range of characters you encountered on a regular basis ensured that dull moments were hard to come by.

I remember one Saturday afternoon being at the gym at the same time as Frank Stallone, brother of Sylvester. After completing his workout he must have stood at the counter for close to an hour, recounting the story of how the original *Rocky* movie came about and how it got made against massive odds. Frank told us that his brother's original intention when it came to casting the part of Apollo Creed had been to use a real fighter, with the likes of Ken Norton and Earnie Shavers auditioning for the role. He went on to regale us with revelations about the background to the movie and how his brother was so broke at the time that he had to sell his dog just to buy groceries.

The relationship between Hollywood and boxing stretches back generations. This is no surprise when you consider that boxing epitomises the struggle of the underdog, and given that the lives of many of its finest and not-so-finest practitioners are steeped in drama, tragedy and personal struggle. Indeed, boxing movies constitute a genre of their own, responsible for more than a few classic and iconic films that have stood the test of time. In the 1950s and 60s, two in particular set the standard. *Requiem For A Heavyweight* (1962) starred Anthony Quinn as the fictional character Harlan 'Mountain' McLintock, a washed-up heavyweight who seeks and finds redemption away from the ring. The original TV version, made in 1956, starred Jack Palance, while a later British TV adaptation made the name of a young Scottish actor called Sean Connery. *Somebody Up There Likes Me* (1956), the story of middleweight legend Rocky Graziano, preceded *Requiem For A Heavyweight*. It starred a young, method-acting Paul Newman.

Moving on, plaudits for the most evocative and realistic boxing movie ever made must go to *Raging Bull* (1980), starring Robert De Niro as the fearsome Jake La Motta. It regularly ranks in critics' all-time top ten movie lists. *The Hurricane* (1999) starring Denzel Washington, dramatising the life of one-time middleweight contender Rubin 'Hurricane' Carter, who fought a long and ultimately successful battle against wrongful imprisonment for murder, is also up there, as is *Cinderella Man* (2005), inspired by the life of Depression-era fighter Jim Braddock, with Russell Crowe in the title role.

Of course any mention of boxing's cinematic history would not be complete without referencing the aforesaid *Rocky* series. It's a series deserving of its own categorisation, and for good and not-so-good reasons. Of the six made at time of writing, only the first and last are worthy of being considered classics – at least in my opinion. The first instalment, as by now well known, was inspired by Ali's 1975 fight against the hitherto anonymous Chuck Wepner. Wepner, a massive underdog, managed to go 15 rounds and succeeded in knocking Ali to the canvas before succumbing to inevitable defeat.

Boxing's depiction on the silver screen proves its merit as a sport that lends itself to the mechanics of storytelling. Anyone who took the time to explore the life and background of even an average fighter in any gym anywhere in the world would understand why. The extreme nature of boxing demands, like all sports do, extraordinary levels of application, dedication, training and discipline if the objective is to succeed. However, the thing that really separates boxing from the vast majority of other sports is that it ultimately involves a willingness to get into a ring to trade punches, with the objective of hurting your opponent more than he can hurt you. The reservoir of mental fortitude and courage required to do so is uncommon. By far the most common source of these qualities, like a river flowing into the sea, is a hard life. The common currency of the majority of fighters is struggle and conflict, a background of dysfunction and hardship of a type your average social worker would be at a loss to comprehend. It is also the stuff of tragedy and drama.

In the modern era, one fighter exemplified more than most a backstory of struggle and hardship. Consequently it was fitting that his was also a story that was later turned into a movie. His name was/is 'Irish' Micky Ward. The movie of his life, *The Fighter*, starred Mark Wahlberg as Ward, whose journey from the streets of Lowell, Massachusetts to boxing glory would be near impossible to believe if it wasn't true.

Fighting at junior welterweight, Ward never held a world title yet still lit up the sport because of the commitment, guts, and excitement he brought to the ring. He turned pro after a successful amateur career that saw him win the New England Golden Gloves title three times. He proceeded to blaze a trail through the professional ranks, winning his first 14 fights, before the wheels came off and he lost his next four. Thereafter, he took a three-year break from the sport before returning to the ring in 1994 and winning nine in a row. This finally brought him the big-name fights he craved and along with them a reputation for courage that has earned him a place in the pantheon of ring legends.

Ward's abiding strength was his durability. Typically, he would soak up punishment until he got the opportunity to land his trademark left hook to the body. It was a style that had already earned him a huge following before he climbed through the ropes in May 2002 to face Canada's Arturo Gatti for the first of the famous trilogy they fought.

Their first fight is rightly considered one of the fights of the century. Broadcast live on HBO, it was a toe-to-toe war that ended in a majority decision in favour of Ward, who immediately agreed to a rematch.

Gatti had done his homework in advance of the second clash, staying low to nullify Ward's body shots while trying to keep him at range. It proved another back-and-forth encounter, with Gatti emerging with the decision on this occasion. Afterwards, Gatti, paying tribute to Ward's tenacity, said: 'I used to wonder what would happen if I fought my twin. Now I know.'

The third and final instalment of Gatti–Ward took place on 7 June 2003 and again produced a classic. As in their previous two encounters, they went to war and in the sixth round Ward scored a knockdown. Gatti was saved by the bell and went on to fight his way to a unanimous decision. At the end, like two men who'd just walked through the bowels of hell together, they hugged one another in acknowledgement of the part they'd just played in making history.

Outside the ring, Micky Ward's life was every bit as incident-packed. A dysfunctional family life, typified by difficult relationships with his mother and older brother, who also boxed, created a rich background that, along with his exploits in the ring, made him a screenwriter's dream. Gatti's tragic death in 2009 added a further Shakespearean quality to the drama of their association, testament to the primordial qualities of a sport that comes closest to stripping away centuries of civilisation to reveal man in the raw.

Any amount of time spent in Hollywood removes any residue of misconception that here resides the glamour and excitement associated with the movie industry. It's a myth to rank with any penned by a Greek tragedian. Most actors struggle to make ends meet with small parts in commercials, TV shows and movies that are so bad their release should be a criminal offence. At Wild Card, there were more than a few bit-part or former actors in this category. Take Jack, for example, a former amateur fighter in his mid-fifties, who trained early mornings when the gym was at its quietest. He would throw a few punches on the bag before stopping to chat for five minutes. Originally from the east coast, every second word that left his mouth was 'fuck' or 'motherfucker'. He'd relocated to LA three decades earlier to establish a career in acting. In that time, his sole claim to fame amounted to a small part in the first *Lethal Weapon* movie.

It was always amusing listening to him talk about his experiences in Hollywood, playing bit parts in various movies and TV shows. It struck me that as much as his career hadn't hit the heights he'd clearly hoped for upon arriving, he'd still had a better existence than one that involved 30 years sitting on your arse in an office turning greyer by the year with the accumulated boredom of conformity.

Macka's fortunes took a turn for the better when he began training Sam Simon, co-creator of the world-famous *Simpsons* cartoon series. Simon liked and appreciated him to the point of giving him a Mercedes as a birthday gift this year – as you do. Macka's services were also regularly used by James Toney, who had him hold the mitts for him a few times a week. When it came to Toney, though, no fee or payment for services rendered was forthcoming. However, Macka's decision to just grin and bear it would pay off when Toney recommended him to the actor James Franco's agent. This after the agent had come looking for someone to train his client for his part in the movie *Annapolis*, which involved boxing scenes. Macka hit it off with him, to the point where he took Macka with him to various movie locations around the world to train and keep him in shape.

Mario Lopez was another Wild Card regular. He'd enjoyed a career as a child actor on a popular US TV sitcom before moving into presenting. He loved boxing, was friends with people like Oscar De La Hoya, and later commentated on various fights for television. In the gym he trained hard and sparred regularly. I never got to know him very well but he exuded the kind of confidence that comes with success. Likewise Scott Caan, son of the actor James Caan and an actor in his own right, was a regular presence. He starred in *Ocean's Eleven* with Brad Pitt and George Clooney before going on to work in various other movies and TV shows. As with Mario Lopez, he sparred regularly, even on occasion with James Toney. When it came to guys like them – the celebrities who trained at Wild Card – it always occurred to me that it was a way of proving to themselves that they were more than spoiled actors or 'Hollywood assholes', feted by an industry in which words like 'honour' and 'pride' have been ripped from the dictionary.

Something that proved popular at the gym around this period were the 'smokers' Freddie decided to organise. These were impromptu boxing cards involving regulars who were non-fighters but wanted to experience what it was like to get in the ring. There was an admission fee and the fights were held under amateur rules – headguards, 14oz gloves, 3 x 2 minute rounds. They were a reflection of the rise in popularity of white-collar boxing, which took off in a big way after the 1999 film *Fight Club* starring Brad Pitt and Ed Norton. In the end Freddie only held two or three of these white-collar events before stopping, realising that if anything went wrong and someone got hurt, he'd be liable. In a city as litigious as LA was, you couldn't blame him.

But the ones that did take place were popular and went a long way to fomenting a sense of fraternity at the gym.

After the last of these 'smokers', Andy, Nick and I drove over to California Chicken on Melrose for a bite to eat. We were buzzing, talking about the fights and venting our critique and opinions of the various guys we'd just witnessed giving it their all. What they lacked in skill they'd made up for in determination. As we were sitting eating and talking, it occurred to me that all three of us had become consumed with the gym and boxing. We were in our mid-thirties – each, if honest, floundering in our respective chosen careers at this point – and Wild Card had provided the sense of purpose and achievement that was lacking in other areas. When we were training and punching the shit out of one another, we felt good about ourselves. Forgotten in the process were the problems awaiting us outside, raising the gym to the status of sanctuary rather than merely a place to go and work out.

But this phase of our lives was coming to an end. Andy, struggling in his efforts to break into acting for a number of years by now, decided it was time to go back to his previous profession of stockbroker. As for Nick, he'd just won a protracted legal battle to regain ownership of his tanning salon from his ex-wife and was intent on focusing his attention on business. As for me, having been in Hollywood for almost five years, it was time to return home.

16

LOCHEND IS a working-class residential area on the east side of Edinburgh, and sitting in the midst of it is the Lochend Boxing Club, housed in an old Scout hut tucked away behind the bend of a nondescript through road.

One cold, dark February evening, I drove all the way over there to take a look. My ears picked up the muted sound of bags being pummelled and that familiar pierce of the buzzer from beyond the door as soon as I pulled up outside. All of a sudden, I was reacquainted with the feeling of butterflies in my stomach. It was a feeling I'd missed in the two years I'd been back in Edinburgh and I was looking forward to enjoying my first proper workout in a long time.

The owner and head trainer at Lochend Boxing Club was Terry McCormack, whom I had met briefly in LA when he was over to liaise with Freddie as part of Alex Arthur's team. Terry had been a decent amateur back in his younger days, but marriage, kids and the pressures of making a living had militated against him making a foray into the pros. Instead, after a few years' absence from the sport, he came back as a trainer. After spending a few years training fighters at various gyms in the city, he managed to gather the resources to open his own place. It had been a struggle to get Lochend up and running and it was a struggle to keep it going. Terry's daily routine when I met him at Lochend consisted of working a full-time job as a binman from 6am until noon, or thereabouts, after which he would head straight to the gym to open up and train fighters all the way through until 9pm, when the place closed. His dedication and commitment was therefore formidable, as it is when it comes to the thousands like him across the world who are the lifeblood and foundation of the sport.

That initial visit to Lochend took place at night, but I soon settled into a pattern of training there in the afternoons, usually three times a week. At Lochend, evenings were taken up by a kids' class, when the place would be packed. Late afternoons were set aside for women, while during daytime the gym was the domain of the pros, up-and-coming amateurs and older keep-fitters like me. The thing every boxing gym needs if it's going to be successful is the right atmosphere. Never mind fancy or expensive equipment and facilities, without the atmosphere to go with it a boxing gym is a soulless and deadening place. In terms of facilities Wild Card, for example, was far from blessed. But in terms of atmosphere it was incomparable, responsible for turning it into a veritable Mecca for boxers from all over the world.

Terry's gym wasn't Wild Card but generated an excellent atmosphere all the same, comprising a combination of promising young fighters, both amateur and pro, guys who were serious about fitness, and a nucleus of people who'd grown up in and around the local community and were bonded tight as a result. The camaraderie meant training there was always something to look forward to. Terry's assistant at the time was John McCarron, a popular character who was always ready with a joke and a smile. He took me on the pads over those first few weeks, letting me know I was nowhere near as fit as I thought I was. You also had characters like Paul Gray, Stevie Laidlaw, Mark Tomassi, Billy Doc, Goags McKenzie and others, ensuring that a visit to Lochend was a riot of banter as much as it was a workout.

By the time I started training at Lochend, Terry was no longer training Alex Arthur.

They'd parted company not long after Alex returned to Scotland from his stint training at Wild Card back in 2003. Terry's stable at the time included Josh Taylor, John Thain, Tommy Philbin, Steven 'Tiff' Tiffney, Gary McMillan and Lewis Benson. I enjoyed watching them spar and train together, bonded tight by a shared dream of establishing successful amateur and then, hopefully, pro careers. Of them all, Josh Taylor was destined to walk through the golden door of boxing fame and fortune.

However, that was still years off in the future at this juncture.

Among the older guys who were training here, a few had boxed competitively as amateurs in their younger years. They retained their connection with the sport by continuing to train to stay in some semblance of shape and helping train the kids at night. The banter alone was worth the drive across to the gym from the other side of the city. Here, if anyone ever made the mistake of believing their shit didn't stink, the illusion was quickly dispelled by a withering verbal assault.

It was probably inevitable that I would start sparring again. I'd been training regularly for six weeks or so when John McCarron asked if I wanted to do a few rounds. I remember I was in the ring shadowboxing, having just started my workout. My automatic response to his invitation was to say yes. But as soon as the word passed from my lips, my stomach tightened with the same old apprehension and dread. It was the same feeling I'd experienced all the way back in the mid-nineties, when I entered that boxing booth in Brussels. It was a feeling I'd experienced many times since, one that never failed to arrive whenever a sparring session loomed.

So I proceeded to climb out of the ring to get ready. Since my hands were already wrapped, all I had to do was spread some vaseline under and over my eyes, on either side of my nose and around my mouth before grabbing a headguard from the cupboard where they were kept. Finally came the task of putting on the requisite 16oz gloves, ensuring with Terry's help that they were fastened nice and tight. 'Here we go again,' is the thought that came to me as I walked back across the gym in the direction of the ring. But just as with every time I'd ever sparred, as soon as I climbed through the ropes the nerves dissipated and in their place arrived adrenalin.

John got into the ring behind me as Terry and most of the others in the gym at the time stopped to watch. It had been a long time but as John and I met in the centre of the ring to touch gloves and get started, I felt good.

Three rounds later, I was all over the place.

Yes, I was doing regular roadwork, able now to do 5k in a respectable time. And, yes, I was capable of doing eight to ten three-minute rounds on the bag in the gym and five to six rounds on the pads. But nothing, absolutely nothing comes close to sparring when it comes to intensity and what it demands and takes out of you. By the middle of the second, I could hardly keep my hands up and John made me pay. The shorter man, you wouldn't have known it from the way he kept popping me with his jab. Worse, every time I threw mine it missed and he countered me with his, invariably followed by a right hand. People were shouting instructions but their words were lost in the chaos. By the end of the round, it was all about survival. Going over to Terry after the buzzer to get some water, I wanted nothing more than to climb out of there.

But I couldn't. It was too late. I had to see it through and take my licks.

'You look nice and relaxed in there,' Terry told me.

I felt anything but relaxed, but his encouragement had a salutary effect all the same. In the next round, I settled down and though still taking the worst of it, I started to land with a few shots of my own. Still, my lack of ring fitness told in the sense that after throwing a combination I found it hard to recover. I tied John up as much as I could in an effort to gain some respite. But then it happened: the hardest punch I've ever been hit with. In all the rounds I'd sparred with Andy and Nick at Wild Card in the years previously, not to mention a few other Wild Card regulars, in all the rounds I'd sparred with Herb and Troy all the way back in the Outlaw Gym days, I had never come close to being knocked out. Nick forced me to take a knee once at Wild Card when he got me with a shot to the solar plexus, but that was it. Apart from that, I'd taken my share of clean shots, some worse than others, but nothing like the one John McCarron caught me with during that first sparring session at Lochend.

I never saw it. It was an overhand right, timed to perfection as I came forward with my left hand down and my chin hanging in the air like my mother's washing. It didn't even hurt on impact. It was just as I'd heard various fighters describe – the punch that KO's you never hurts. It certainly put me to sleep for a second. A white curtain descended and I completely forgot where I was. Then it cleared and I felt myself wobble. All this seemed to take a long time as the fog in my brain cleared, while in truth lasting mere seconds. John was standing a few feet away. After giving me a few seconds to recover, he came forward again. I got him in what I'm guessing was the tightest clinch he's ever been in. I was desperate for the buzzer. I was out on my feet and all I could do was cling on. It's amazing how time can become the single most important thing in your life when you're in a state of emergency. Every second passed like an hour before thankfully, at last, the buzzer went to signal the end of the round.

My immediate thought was to get out of there and find a quiet spot to lie down in. I was hoping against hope that either John or Terry would say that's enough and bring this public execution to an end. No such luck. Terry administered the water and said, 'One more?'

'Aye,' John replied.

Terry looked at me. I had no choice. I had to say yes. Three more minutes of hell was on the way. If I'd respected boxers before, now I worshipped them. Nothing I had ever been through, excepting a broken neck, came close.

John was tiring by this stage too and for the first minute of the third, the two of us were content to stand off, throwing the odd punch. There was no real purpose behind mine at this point, no determination to win or make him pay for his earlier punch. But that's exactly what I did when he came forward behind a listless jab. On instinct alone, I threw a left-right combination. As he'd done to me in the previous round, I caught him flush on the way in, achieving that irresistible double impact. He stepped back shouting, 'Good shot mate!'

His right eye had exploded into an ugly mound of pus beneath a massive black bruise. He tried to regroup but the fight had been taken out of him and he was reduced to bluffing. It wasn't the time to press forward and so, just as he did with me, I laid off to give him time to recover and get his bearings. This is how the sparring session ended.

I climbed out of the ring euphoric with relief. It's always the same after going through the gruelling ordeal of a hard spar – you emerge feeling ten feet tall over the fact you have overcome your fears and emerged intact. John remained in the ring working on the heavy bruise underneath his eye with the small iron that was kept beneath the counter for that very purpose and which someone had fetched for him.

I would be lying if I did not admit to being determined never to put myself through the experience again. The right hand John McCarron hit me with I would not soon forget, and for days afterwards I could hardly think of anything else. This is what happens when you start sparring; it begins to dominate your thoughts. When you're away from the gym all you think about is the next session to come, while afterwards you find yourself running the last sparring session over and over, dissecting it as if it was the most important thing you have ever done or would ever do.

I went on to spar with John McCarron many more times after that. I also enjoyed some hard sparring with Paul Gray, who could hit, and even with Terry himself, who once put me down with a shot to the solar plexus. While I could never claim to have ever reached a level of proficiency commensurate with the word skilled, I did relish the opportunity that regular sparring provided to improve.

An interesting aspect of boxing is the way it has thrown up a liberal sprinkling of fighters who've had to overcome a lack of natural ability to succeed. Not every world champion who's ever laced up the gloves was endowed with a surfeit of natural, God-given talent for the sport. One of the most prominent examples in this regard is Britain's Chris Eubank. In 1988, when he was still a novice professional, the flamboyant middleweight opined, 'If you want the truth, I started boxing because the South Bronx was a place of nightmares. I hid away in the gymnasium because I hated it out there. I trained like a maniac to get out of that place and here I am a world-class professional athlete in my opinion and looking for a good promoter.' Five years later, his fortunes and success in the sport had improved to the point where he felt able to boast, 'I used to steal suits for a living, now I pay a grand for them.'

It was no idle boast, for by then Eubank had elevated himself to being the most talked-about, controversial and exciting fighter in British boxing – perhaps even the most exciting athlete in the country in any sport. Not only was he a regular fixture on the back pages of the nation's newspapers, he was a regular feature on the front pages too. He held, also, the distinction of being one of the most controversial personalities in the country, partly due to his strutting ring entrances to a cacophony of boos and jeers from packed audiences willing to part with their hard-earned cash in the hope of seeing him get knocked out.

The man, in sum, was a promotional and marketing genius.

His two fights against Nigel Benn have yet to be equalled when it comes to drama and courage in a British boxing ring, and it is arguable that only Ali–Frazier and Leonard–Hearns have eclipsed the rivalry they shared, one in which no quarter was asked or given. Eubank emerged victorious after their first fight at Birmingham's National Exhibition Centre in 1990, when Richard Steele stepped in during the ninth round to save Benn from taking any more punishment in what had been a ring war. During the customary post-fight interviews, Eubank could hardly speak he was in so much pain, having suffered a broken rib and a damaged tongue.

Between that epic battle and the next one they fought in 1993 at Manchester United's Old Trafford, which ended in a draw in front of 40,000 fans and a mammoth television audience of 16 million, Eubank enhanced his reputation with a series of wins against the likes of Gary Stretch, Michael Watson (twice), Thulani Malinga, Tony Thornton and Ray Close. By now, his ring walk to Tina Turner's 'Simply The Best' had become part of the legend, as was his habit of jumping over the top rope into the ring and strutting and preening like a gladiator, soaking up the energy of sold-out arenas wherever he fought.

Outside the ring, eccentricity was his stock-in-trade; Eubank adopted the mannerisms and demeanour of an English country gent, replete with jodhpurs, monocle and cane. In this respect he was a throwback to Jack Johnson, another boxing dandy who confounded, shocked and entertained the public with his refusal to act and behave in the manner expected of a black world champion.

Eubank, in sum, was a sportswriter's dream and an extremely clever fighter to boot, reflected in the unprecedented eight-fight £10 million contract he signed with Sky Sports in the mid-1990s. It was money the Brighton-based champion used to finance an exorbitant lifestyle – mansions, top-of-the-range cars, an expensive wardrobe, motorcycles and even the biggest truck in Europe at the time. It was a spending spree that, along with a spate of dodgy investments, ended in him going bankrupt in 2005.

But even without the toys and the money, one thing no one will ever be able to take away from Chris Eubank is his legacy as one of the most courageous and proud champions to grace British boxing. The opponents on his record comprise a who's who of the most illustrious middleweights and super middleweights this country has ever produced. Adding to Nigel Benn and Michael Watson are the names of Steve Collins and Joe Calzaghe. It shouldn't be forgotten either that Eubank fought the first three not once but twice.

Eubank's last meaningful contest came against a much bigger and stronger Carl Thompson in 1998, in the second of two challenges he mounted that year against the formidable Manchester-born champion for his WBO cruiserweight title. Eubank lost the first fight by a 12-round unanimous decision, while the second saw him go out on his shield in the ninth round. His performance that night still ranks as one of the most extraordinary displays of courage ever seen in a ring. The standing ovation he received at the end was all that he deserved. After a long career suffused with controversy and drama, Eubank had succeeded in winning over a hard-to-please British boxing public that now, at the end, embraced him as a warrior who'd given them many such nights of thrills and spills.

Staying with this theme, John Conteh is a name inextricably linked not only with British boxing but British culture in the 1970s. A ubiquitous presence on the chat show circuit and on television in his pomp, the handsome Scouser rose to prominence on the back of a resurgent British working class. On television, on stage, in movies, music, politics and sports, the 1970s was the last decade of the working man before Thatcher unleashed her right-wing revolution in the 1980s, upending in the process the collectivist ethos that had held sway in the country since the Second World War. She replaced it with rampant individualism and greed as the country's dominant cultural values. With his strong working-class roots, movie star looks and prodigious boxing skills, Conteh was one of the decade's pin-ups. At the height of his fame, he even appeared on the cover of Paul McCartney's *Band On The Run* album.

He started boxing when he was 10 at a local amateur club in Kirkby. At 19, representing England, he took the light-heavyweight gold medal at the 1970 Commonwealth Games in Edinburgh. Turning pro after the Games, he fought 26 times before challenging for the world title in 1974 against Jorge Ahumada, a tough Argentinian who most writers and commentators felt would be too much for the Liverpudlian. But Conteh confounded the naysayers by defeating Ahumada over 15 hard rounds to take the belt on points in front of a packed crowd at Wembley Arena.

In terms of style, he was easy on the eye, combining an excellent jab with sharp combinations and superb reflexes, making up for in pure boxing skill what he lacked in power. Prior to winning the light-heavyweight world title, he was involved in one of the all-time classic domestic fights in 1973, when as European champion he took on and defeated the then British and Commonwealth champion Chris Finnegan.

Conteh at his peak was Britain's answer to Muhammad Ali and many indeed touted him as a potential future opponent of the heavyweight legend, even though if he'd actually gone up a division to face him he would've done so as one of the smallest heavyweights ever. When considering John Conteh's career now, decades later, the impression left is of a supremely gifted fighter who ruined his legacy upon taking the title by falling for the lure of nightclubs and parties, drowning his talent and discipline in hedonism. Yet on the way up, his spartan training regimen was legendary, involving mammoth sparring sessions, hill runs and regular swims in freezing cold water to develop the mental and physical toughness he was known for. Like most hungry young fighters, he lived in the gym, where he applied himself to the task in the knowledge that boxing offered him a route out of poverty.

After winning the world title in 1974, Conteh's fame went through the roof, his looks and charisma responsible for seeing him transcend the sport to become a household name. He successfully defended his title three times before he was stripped of it for pulling out of a mandatory defence against Miguel Cuello two days before the fight. In 1977, he attempted to regain his belt but lost to Mate Parlov, the Yugoslavian champion, in a controversial 15-round split decision in Belgrade. Conteh fought a further six times before retiring in 1980, after his licence was revoked on medical grounds, with a record of 34 wins, one draw and four defeats.

Thereafter, he embarked on a career in show business. However, an addiction to alcohol saw him follow the sad but common path of ex-fighters who, after achieving fame and wealth in the ring, go on to self-destruct in retirement. Yet in his case, refusing to be vanquished, he successfully battled his alcoholism and went on to enjoy a second career on the after-dinner speaking circuit, while also finding the time for charity work. Younger boxing fans unfamiliar with John Conteh would be doing themselves a favour by searching out footage of the Liverpudlian in action when he was in his pomp.

17

AROUND SIX months after I started training at Lochend, Alex Arthur walked through the door. It was the first time I'd seen him since LA, though I'd continued to follow his career. Since losing to Michael Gomez in their classic encounter in 2003, Alex had gone on to enjoy renewed success followed by further setback. He initially came back to win the British, Commonwealth and European titles at super featherweight, before taking the interim WBO world title in 2007 after stopping a tough Georgian southpaw, Koba Gogoladze, in the tenth round of a hard-fought contest in Cardiff. He successfully defended his interim title against Englishman Steve Foster later that year in Edinburgh, in what turned out to be one of the toughest fights of his career, during which the challenger knocked him through the ropes in the 11th round.

Soon thereafter, Alex was awarded the full title when the reigning champion, Juan Guzman, chose to vacate rather than defend it. Alex then went on to face London's Nicky Cook at the MEN Arena in Manchester in his first title defence. I recall in the build-up to the fight how emaciated and weak he looked. It was clear that making super featherweight had taken a massive toll, to the point where at the weigh-in he appeared as if he was ready to collapse. That he was able to make it to the ring, much less fight, was a feat in itself. He told me later that he'd never felt so ill as he did on the day of the weigh-in, and that by fight night was all but done in. What ensued was a unanimous points decision in favour of Cook. Alex disputed the decision afterwards, however watching the fight it was hard to disagree with. In truth Alex had been defeated less by Cook and more by the scales, paying the price for failing to move up in weight after outgrowing super featherweight. He would later tell me that he'd wanted to relinquish the title and move up, but had been promised a big money fight against Mexican legend Marco Antonio Barrera if he stayed at super feather and came through against Nicky Cook. Looked at from this angle you couldn't blame him for rolling the dice. After all, most people in and around the sport at the time felt that he would defeat Cook comfortably, given their respective resumes.

Entering a ring to engage in unarmed combat wearing 8 or 10oz gloves is dangerous enough. Doing so half starved and malnourished skirts the limits of survival, inviting not only defeat against a stronger and more nourished opponent, but death. Of the far too many fatalities that have littered the sport, a lack of food, fluids and sustenance has played its part. Fighters starving and dehydrating themselves in order to make weight is an arcane throwback to a bygone age, pre sports science and pre proper regulation and oversight.

Anyway, it was after the Cook fight that Alex Arthur and Terry McCormack resumed their partnership, with Alex determined to regain a world title sooner rather than later. His presence in the gym gave the younger fighters like John Thain and Josh Taylor a lift, allowing them to see what it was that had brought him the success he'd enjoyed. He in turn benefited from their enthusiasm and hunger. Watching him spar with Thain and Taylor never failed to remind me of the time I watched him spar at Wild Card years previously. The countless rounds of sparring a professional fighter completes in an average career is remarkable, testament to the human spirit when fuelled by a desire to succeed.

Interspersed with sessions at the gym, I was still doing roadwork three or four times a week. Typically, this took the form of 30- to 40-minute runs close to where I lived on the west side of the city. The two routes I went could never be described as picturesque, each taking me along streets heavy with traffic and the jarring noise and activity of the inner city. One of the routes included an industrial estate. Regardless, I ran religiously and only ever took time off if I was injured or in the depths of winter when there was ice on the ground. In all my years of training, I have never found anything that comes close to running for the feeling of wellbeing you experience afterwards. It's a cleansing sensation, as if walking on a bed of air, which is why if I had to choose one single exercise over any other, it would be running.

Whenever I felt like a change of scenery, I would jump in the car, drive over to Arthur's Seat and run there. An ancient volcanic rock to the east of the city centre, Arthur's Seat is one of Edinburgh's most iconic landmarks, standing resolute for centuries throughout the myriad convulsions and events that have mapped both the city and country's history. The panoramic view of Edinburgh from the top is simply magnificent. It is enjoyed by hillwalkers, fitness enthusiasts and people out for a stroll around its circumference of just over three miles, much of it involving a challenging hill climb in either direction. It makes for an excellent training run for athletes and fitness buffs, and I lost count of the number of hours I spent running here. In many ways, it was Edinburgh's answer to Runyon Canyon in Hollywood, weather apart. Sometimes, when I felt like pushing myself harder, I would take the steep, rough path that runs up and round one side of the crags. It was a route that certainly got you in touch with your inner child, requiring considerable determination to make it up and over the other side without stopping. In my case, it required monumental determination to make it.

18

ANOTHER REGULAR face at Lochend Boxing Club was Ken Buchanan, Scotland's most famous fighter and a true legend of the ring. Growing up in Edinburgh, I was aware of Ken from a young age. I retained a vague memory of watching him fight Jim Watt for the British lightweight title with my dad in the tiny living room of our council flat back in 1973. Little did I know that by the time he fought and defeated Watt over 15 tough rounds at the St Andrew's Sporting Club in Glasgow, his best days were already behind him.

Comparing the fortunes of Ken Buchanan and Jim Watt in retirement is to undertake a study in the turbulence of life. Whereas Buchanan, who earned the kind of accolades Watt could only dream about when he was fighting, found life after boxing more difficult than he'd probably ever anticipated, Watt went on to establish a second career as a successful pundit and commentator. Indeed, he seemed to move seamlessly from life inside the ring to the much tougher one for most boxers outside it. Watt as a fighter was no slouch, a holder of the world lightweight title no less, but he wasn't in the same class as Buchanan, and to be fair to him he never claimed that he was.

One of the more disagreeable aspects of the Scottish working-class psyche is a tendency to relish the misfortune of others. This is especially the case when it involves those who manage to achieve considerable success, only to later fall on hard times. Jealousy, envy, a need to justify a comparative lack of achievement in their own lives: who knows what lies at the root of such a malign national trait? But it was never more in evidence than in the case of Buchanan, who found himself subjected to disrespect and disregard from some people who'd never come close to touching the greatness he had, and who never would. What recognition he did receive probably came too late to completely heal the emotional scars he carried over the way his victory against legendary Panamanian Ismael Laguna in Puerto Rico, which earned him the world title in September 1970, was received back home.

Imagine after winning such a titanic 15-round battle in 100-degree heat, on the back of a performance that will forever be prefixed with the word 'superhuman', returning home to be greeted at the airport by just a smattering of wellwishers. It wasn't as if Scotland had produced a long line of world champions in the years prior to Buchanan's success. On the contrary, here was a small nation unused to success in *any* individual sport, never mind the hardest one of all.

But no matter the lack of appreciation his achievements in the ring met with from the powers that be in his home city, around the world Ken will always be a legend, especially in America. This was no surprise considering that in his peak in the early 1970s, he was the uncrowned king of Madison Square Garden. The acknowledged Mecca of boxing in its heyday, the Garden was where ring legends were made, confirmed and also destroyed. Even the most accomplished of champions and contenders were at risk of being overwhelmed by the pressure of performing in front of the most knowledgeable and hard-to-please fans in the world. More than any other arena, the Garden is synonymous with boxing. Its close association with the sport is due to the 100 years and four different locations in which it has hosted fights involving a who's who of boxing royalty – the likes of John L. Sullivan, Rocky Marciano, Sugar Ray Robinson, Jake La Motta, Muhammad Ali, Jerry Quarry, Joe Frazier, Roberto Duran and Sugar Ray Leonard. This makes it all the more remarkable that Ken Buchanan, product of a housing estate in Edinburgh, fought and topped the bill there five times in his career.

His first appearance at the Garden in his trademark tartan/plaid shorts came three months after that epic victory over Laguna in 1970. He fought a tough Canadian welterweight contender, Donato Paduano, in a ten-round non-title fight. Giving away ten pounds in bodyweight to his opponent, Buchanan lit up the crowd to such an extent that it rose more than once to give him a standing ovation in appreciation of the sheer artistry he displayed in taking Paduano apart. Ducking and weaving to avoid punches, it was as if his body was attached to his legs by a ball and socket instead of flesh and bone. At points, he dipped his head so low he could have untied the Canadian's laces and in the end ran out a comfortable winner by unanimous decision. Buchanan's next outing at the Garden came the following year in a widely anticipated rematch against Ismael Laguna. Buchanan had already defended his title twice, establishing himself as the undisputed champion, and the rematch against Laguna took on the same pattern as their first encounter. Ken kept his jab in the Panamanian's face for 15 rounds on the way to winning another unanimous decision in front of a full house.

Another Panamanian in the shape of a young Roberto Duran was Buchanan's next challenger at the Garden. Duran may only just have been emerging as the legend he was to become but he already possessed a reputation for destroying his opponents with a relentless, come-forward style, throwing bombs. It was a fight that none who saw it would ever forget and remains one of the most controversial that Madison Square Garden has ever been host to. It started at a blistering pace from the opening bell, when Duran literally tried to jump on Buchanan in order to nullify a jab that by then was considered the best in the business. It was a strategy that paid off as within a minute of the first round,

Buchanan was forced to touch the canvas after taking a right hook. If he didn't know it already, the world champion knew now that he was in for a long night.

Back he came, though, trading combinations with the younger man in an attempt to keep him at bay. It was in this fashion the fight continued over 13 bruising rounds during which Duran's head rarely left Buchanan's chest, so intent was he on fighting on the inside.

The low blow that concluded proceedings came after the bell at the end of the 13th. The resulting controversy continues to be the subject of debate to this day. More importantly, it still rankles with Buchanan himself, who by his own account was still being reminded of the punch years later by the occasional shooting pain passing through his groin. The blow was clearly low, as anyone watching the fight would attest to, and it clearly came after the bell, leaving the champion flat on the canvas unable to continue. However, rather than disqualify Duran for a low blow, the fight was awarded to the Panamanian challenger on the basis that he'd been ahead on all three judges' scorecards at the time and that, in the referee's opinion, the blow had landed just above the belt. Duran refused to grant Buchanan a rematch afterwards and always considered the Scotsman one of his toughest opponents.

Ken Buchanan fought twice more at the Garden after that, recording victories against former three-time world champion Carlos Ortiz and then South Korea's Chang-Kil Lee.

It was hard to square the unparalleled heights Buchanan reached inside the ring with the man who would regularly pop up at Lochend. Sometimes he would hit the bag for a few rounds but mostly he would just spend a couple of hours chatting with Terry and the guys while watching a new generation of talent training in the hope of achieving a fraction of the success he'd enjoyed. There were no airs and graces about him, nothing at all to suggest greatness, and he neither sought nor expected to be feted by anyone. Nature had endowed him with the genetic make-up of a piece of string, ensuring that he carried the same dimensions as the young man who had met Ismael Laguna on a blisteringly hot afternoon in San Juan, Puerto Rico all those years ago.

It was always a pleasure listening to him talk about his life and career. He talked about the time Ali was on the undercard of his fight with Paduano. A member of Ali's entourage asked if Ali could share his dressing room and, saying yes, Ken grabbed a piece of chalk and drew a line across the floor before jokingly telling him that Ali could have one half while he would take the other, warning him to make sure that nobody from his entourage crossed the line. He talked about what it was like to fight Duran and how he'd met the ring legend at a few boxing events in the years since. It was like listening to a living encyclopaedia of boxing, and many would have undoubtedly paid for the privilege.

Ultimately, the kind of greatness Ken Buchanan achieved is rare in any sport, much less boxing.

19

IT STARTED innocuously enough.

I was finishing my workout, sitting on the ring apron resting between sets of abdominal crunches, when Terry came over and asked me if I'd be up for devising a programme to help John Thain build power in his legs.

Terry was aware of my experience as a bodybuilder and with John having just recently turned pro, he needed to increase his all-round body strength and power. I told him, yes. I did not realise it would mark the start of a two-year stint in the unofficial role of John's strength and conditioning coach.

It came to me early on that the only way I could help John to build up his legs was if I actually put him through the programme, rather than merely write it down for him to do by himself. I relayed the suggestion to Terry over the phone and he was enthusiastic. Afterwards, I called John and arranged to meet him at the gym that coming Saturday for his first leg workout.

However, on the Friday beforehand, I walked into the gym and as soon as I laid eyes on him realised that before he could even think about working to increase the strength in his legs, and with it the power in his punches, John would have to pay attention to his diet. His physique bore all the evidence of being in a catabolic state, wherein his body, starved of nutrition, was feeding on its own muscle tissue for the protein it required to deal with the stress he was putting on it in training. While this was bad enough for a normal person, for an athlete it was disastrous.

That night I called him and explained the situation. The amount of calories he was ingesting needed to double as a matter of urgency. In addition, I instructed him to start taking four high-quality protein shakes every day and reduce the length of time he was spending in the gym to an hour per workout. I explained to him that he had to start viewing his metabolism as a furnace which needed to be constantly fuelled to work efficiently and that a high intake of protein was needed for recovery and to maintain a positive nitrogen balance, so that when the muscle tissue in his body that had been broken down during training needed protein to repair and recover, it would be there.

John's hunger to succeed dictated that he was willing to do whatever it took to improve. He listened, took on board my advice, and without hesitation followed it. Instead of starting the leg workout on the Saturday, as originally arranged, I told him to spend the weekend resting and eating, suggesting that we start the leg programme early the following week. Before speaking to John, I'd already spoken with Terry, who agreed with my analysis of the situation and the way to proceed. We were in business.

I'd never trained anyone prior to John. In my years as an active bodybuilder, I'd helped or advised many people on their training and nutrition, but never in an organised or sustained fashion. Training to add muscle for cosmetic effect, as in bodybuilding, and training for the speed and power a boxer needs in the ring, obviously constitute two completely different objectives that require two contrasting approaches. My years at Wild Card, where I was introduced to plyometrics by Justin, would come in handy, as would my long experience of training with weights. My intention from the outset was to combine both.

Initially, the workout I devised for John centred around heavy squats, the king of all power exercises. In order to make it sport-specific for an athlete who needs to combine power and speed, I had him pause at the bottom of each rep before exploding up on command. This would make each rep harder and emphasise the use of the muscle's fast twitch fibres – vital when it came to generating explosive power. I combined squats with various plyometric movements with the medicine ball, again with the objective of developing his fast twitch muscle fibres. In time, I would develop and change the sessions to focus more on speed throughout the execution of the movement, dropping the heavy squats and moving more in the direction of pure velocity and plyometric work.

For those who don't know, plyometrics – or plyos – is a form of exercise designed to build explosive strength. Each movement involves a quick explosion from a dead or stationary position to the end point. Examples of plyo exercises for the legs are bounding, standing base jumps and block jumps. For the upper body, a variety of explosive press-up type movements, high-velocity movements and pushing movements with barbells and dumbbells provide best results. Back in the Wild Card days, Justin would take a group of us through various strength and conditioning routines that were heavily focused on the aforementioned movements and exercises. He would set up two thick wooden blocks on the floor in parallel to one another. They were each around six inches high. He then had us lie prone on the floor in the classic press-up position in front of the block, prior to going through various explosive drills. Those involved pushing up from the floor and landing on top of the blocks with one or both hands at the same time, moving between blocks with one hand landing on the floor and the other on top, and so on. It was hard work and if you managed four or five reps on each movement, you were doing well.

The crucial thing when it came to plyometrics was to ensure that you ended a given set before the point of exhaustion. As soon as you began to slow down, it was imperative to stop. Muscle memory is the key and for boxers whose discipline requires explosive power and speed, it's essential that the muscles become accustomed to moving at speed and with dynamic power in training, so as to prepare them to do the same in the ring.

20

I RETURNED to Wild Card on a two-week visit in late 2009, four years after leaving and nine years after moving to Hollywood to start a new life. As I sat back on the aircraft at Heathrow Airport and buckled up in my seat before take-off, my mind took me back to those days. I thought about Andy and big Nick. I thought about Freddie's brother, Pep, and about Macka, Boris, Alex and Troy. I wondered if I would find them still there or whether they'd moved on. I described earlier the misfortune that befell Nigel. One of the first things I intended to do upon getting to LA was go and visit him. I'd asked Andy during a phone conversation before flying out if Nigel was still living in the same apartment, where we used to gather to watch the big fights. Andy said he wasn't sure. It didn't matter; I would find out soon enough. If not, I would make an effort to track him down. I'd never forgotten the way Nigel extended the hand of friendship when I first arrived at the gym in 2000. I recall the year he spent Christmas Day with me and my girlfriend at the time.

I liked him at lot and my heart ached over the tragedy that had beset him.

Speaking of Andy, his fortunes had undergone a drastic transformation during the time I'd been gone. Prior to my departure at the start of 2005, he'd been in the process of moving out of his friend Jimmy's apartment into a small place of his own. I helped him move in, donating a couple of pieces of furniture I no longer needed as I myself was in the process of packing up and leaving LA at the time. Four years on, after deciding to give up his dream of an acting career in Hollywood to return to his previous job as a stockbroker, he was enjoying considerable success – at least if what he'd been telling me over the phone about the big house he'd just moved into and the cars he owned were anything to go by. He no longer trained at Wild Card, having decided to follow Justin to the gym he'd opened a few miles away after parting company with Freddie to go his own way.

As for Nick, according to Andy he'd stopped boxing altogether, concentrating all of his time and energy on his various business interests instead. I'd arranged to meet up with Andy during my trip and I was also hoping to visit Justin's new gym and catch up with him too. All in all, it was shaping up to be an interesting trip.

Arriving at LAX, I collected the car I'd booked for the duration and headed up to Hollywood via the 405 North and 10 East freeways. It was early evening and in the distance the Hollywood Hills were framed in a red sky as the sun dipped behind them. It lifted my spirits; the old feelings of hope and opportunity with which this part of the world is associated returning as I bowled along the freeway. I turned up the volume on the R&B station I was listening to and began tapping the steering wheel to the beat. Yes, I thought, I'm back.

I was staying at a youth hostel in West Hollywood, having booked it online attracted by the reasonable rates and facilities that I'd been assured by the manager of the place, when calling in advance, were decent. I'd booked a single room, which I was relieved to find was spacious and clean. I did not anticipate I would be spending much time there, but I was still unprepared for the parties held downstairs in the bar on a nightly basis that went on into the wee small hours. I wasn't the oldest guest staying there but I was close, the experience taking me back to my first prolonged stop in LA in 1992, when in my early twenties I'd stayed at a hostel close to Venice Beach and thought the world was my oyster. I was a different animal then, still to be bitten by life and its ups and downs, full of hope, expectation and belief in the wonderous possibilities it offered. Age and experience has a habit of blunting a man's dreams.

Next morning I woke early and ventured out for coffee. The rumble of traffic on Melrose Avenue assailed my ears as I took up a seat in the veranda of the coffee shop I'd happened upon. From here I spent the next half hour watching the world go by. It was still too early to hit the gym, so I decided to kill the time getting reacquainted with the city. The only downside to this trip was that I wouldn't get to see Freddie. He was training Manny Pacquiao in the Philippines for his upcoming fight against Miguel Cotto and wasn't due back in LA for another three weeks. Pacquiao had risen to become a ring phenomenon in the intervening years. He was in the midst of a run of emphatic victories at different weights, earning him a massive international following and lending him an aura of invincibility that had elevated his status in the sport to something even more than iconic. In the Philippines he was a national hero and there was talk of him going into politics (which he would do the following year, when he was elected on his second attempt as a congressman to the Filipino House of Representatives) and eventually even becoming the nation's president. His last fight had been against Britain's Ricky Hatton, another fighter with a huge following, who had previously lost to the only boxer whom it was felt stood a chance of defeating Pacquiao in the ring, Floyd Mayweather Jr.

Speaking of Hatton, such was the devastating second-round KO he'd suffered against Pacquiao in 2009, many were calling for him to retire. Ricky, at the time in question, had yet to make any decision on his future. Proud warrior that he was, he'd always made it clear that his goal in boxing was to test himself against the best. It is why he never ducked anybody and one of the reasons he was so respected and lionised in the UK. Hatton was a throwback to the days when pride and honour were just as important a motive force as money in a professional fighter's outlook.

Assuming he didn't need the money after his involvement in two fights that were among the most lucrative to have taken place in many years, the question was whether Hatton still hankered for the buzz? The lure of the ring for a Ricky Hatton or a Muhammad Ali or a Sugar Ray Leonard was as hard to resist as a crackpipe is for a drug addict. The glory, the limelight, the purpose that comes with preparing for a big fight, the thrill of performing in front of thousands of people – millions when you take into account television and the wider media – all combine to make retirement much harder for many elite and top fighters than fighting.

It was this inability to let go that saw Oscar De La Hoya fight on past his prime and suffer a humiliating loss against the same man who brutally knocked out Hatton – Manny Pacquiao. Boxing is the greatest sport in the world but also the most cruel, exemplifying courage, artistry and brutality in equal measure. It straddles the line between nobility and barbarity, pitting two men of roughly equal size and weight against one another in ritualised and legal unarmed combat. Sadly, at times the nobility is not easy to find, lost in the greed, venality and dishonesty that has come to be associated with the professional game. It is why a champion like Pacquiao had given the sport a much-needed injection of integrity. Here was a fighter of genuine dignity who treated everyone he came into contact with, including his opponents, with respect. Boxing benefited from having a world champion who didn't talk trash and deride or denigrate all and sundry, who didn't brag about the money he was making, the cars he owned, who hadn't succumbed to the bling culture that was increasingly commonplace, turning it into an ugly mirror of the excesses of Western culture and values.

Ricky Hatton, likewise, was a fighter from humble origins who'd never allowed fame and success to distort his worldview.

Four years on, the fortunes of both men since sharing a ring in Las Vegas in May 2009 proved the wisdom implicit in the statement, 'Fortune knocks but once, but misfortune has much more patience.'

After admitting to battling depression after his loss to Pacquiao and with his flirtation with cocaine and descent into binge drinking plastered all over the papers – evidence of the abiding cruelty and vindictiveness of the British tabloid press – Hatton declared his intention to return to the ring in 2012. He had unfinished business, he said, and was determined to try to redeem the devastating defeat against Pacquiao that initially ended his career.

Evidence that the former world champion remained a popular figure in the UK was provided by the headlines his comeback announcement commanded. It was the top item on every news channel and front page in the same newspapers that had gone out of their way to humiliate Hatton over his cocaine use previously. Regardless, the stage appeared set for a return of the glory days.

But alas it wasn't to be. The Mancunian went down to a body shot in the ninth round against the Ukrainian

Vyacheslav Senchenko at a sold-out Manchester Arena. Some felt afterwards that Ricky should have faced a lesser opponent in his first fight back after being out for over three years. But with the kind of honesty and straight talking that had endeared him to millions, he said at the post-fight press conference he knew it wasn't there any more. Hatton said that he could kid himself on and try to make excuses, but he refused to deny the truth and was finally calling it a day. Since then, he's been a ubiquitous presence around the sport as a pundit, promoter and manager. He trains young fighters and top contenders at his gym and seems to be in a good place. Long may it continue.

As for Manny Pacquiao, the sustained aura of invincibility he enjoyed was shattered by two back-to-back defeats in the same year, 2012, as Hatton's return to the ring. The first was a controversial points defeat to Timothy Bradley, a fight that everyone bar the judges believed Pacquiao won convincingly. If that result was controversial, the second of his defeats in 2012 could not have been more emphatic. It came at the hands of his ring nemesis, Juan Manuel Marquez, in one of the most brutal and frightening knockouts you will ever see in the squared circle. In fact, to describe the way Manny hit the canvas as a knockout is to engage in understatement. He was floored like a man who'd just been hit head-on by a truck at full speed. Watching him bounce off the canvas unconscious sent a chill down my spine, and as he lay there inert I'm sure I speak for many in saying I feared he wouldn't be getting up again, ever. Fortunately, though, he was back on his feet after a minute or so and did not suffer serious or permanent damage from the KO – at least not in the short term – and was able to fight again. If anyone felt that fighters like Manny Pacquiao were overpaid, this one brutal moment in his fourth encounter with the tough Mexican – the only one of Pacman's fifty-odd opponents to have had his number up to that point – would have dispelled the notion once and for all. One thing that did appear certain was an end to any talk of the much-anticipated and yearned-for superfight between Manny and Floyd Mayweather, which fans of the sport had been calling for and hoping to see for a long time. On the contrary, as with Hatton, the consensus now was that Manny should retire and focus on his by now busy political career in the Philippines. Yet, remarkably, not only did he manage to come back from such a devastating loss, he looked impressive, handing tough contender Brandon Rios a 12-round lesson in speed, accuracy and power in November 2013 when they clashed in Macau, China. He followed it up with the demolition of Timothy Bradley in their rematch in early 2014, along with the rolling over of Chris Algieri later the same year. All of a sudden, clarion calls for that long-anticipated superfight against Mayweather started up again, proving that boxing is as unpredictable and changeable as a summer's day in Scotland.

21

I PARKED on Lillian Way, the sidestreet at the back of the Wild Card parking lot where I always used to park back in the day. The gym's parking lot was small and tight and difficult to manoeuvre in and out of, and from experience it was usually packed. I'd rarely parked there in the years I lived in Hollywood and saw no reason to change now.

It was a surreal feeling to be back after four years' absence. As I entered the parking lot through the gate in the boundary fence, I automatically cast my eyes up to the entrance of the gym at the top of the stone stairs leading up to it, where as ever a group of guys were standing chatting. Sets of hand wraps were hanging over the rail, drying in the sun after use, and the familiar sounds of a boxing gym in full swing grew louder as I approached. It had been some time since my adrenalin had run so intensely, and climbing the stairs there was no doubting the fact that I'd missed this place.

I entered to be met by the same scene of chaos and energy I left at the start of 2005. A quick scan picked out a few faces from back then, while noting that the layout of the gym hadn't changed much either – apart, that is, from the extension through the back, where a second boxing ring had been established, along with some weights and other sundry equipment. Most of the heavy bags were just as I remembered them, as were the myriad pictures, newspaper clippings and boxing memorabilia that covered the walls.

Overall, it felt as if I'd never been away, a feeling enhanced when Pep Roach came over, shook my hand and said, 'Where the fuck have you been?'

It was good to see him and we spent the next few minutes chatting at the counter. As we did, in walked Craig McEwan. Craig, as I mentioned earlier, was from Clovenstone in Edinburgh. He was a southpaw fighting at middleweight who'd made the move to LA in 2006 at the end of a long amateur career consisting of over 350 fights, during which he represented Scotland at two Commonwealth Games. Rather than turn pro at home in the UK, he came out here to see if he could impress Freddie Roach with a view to embarking on his pro career Stateside. Freddie took a look at him and, duly impressed, agreed to train him, while also arranging for Craig to be signed to Oscar De La Hoya's Golden Boy Promotions. In summary, Craig McEwan's start in the pros couldn't have been better, to the point where his head must have been spinning at the direction his life had taken. This kind of thing generally didn't happen to people from Clovenstone, and the distance he'd travelled was one that couldn't be measured in air miles alone. Craig, after three years, had put together an undefeated record of 16-0. We'd met briefly in Edinburgh before, when I'd spent a few weeks training at his father Rab's gym, and it was good to see him again. About to leave for a training camp in Canada, where he was fighting next, he seemed focused.

Another fighter I ran into during the trip was Ola Afolabi, whose fortunes had likewise undergone a huge transformation. When I first knew him, he was a kid with bags of potential who, as I've already recounted, seemed to spend more time larking around the gym than training. I retained memories of the early-morning runs we used to go on in the same group at Griffith Park, organised by Justin Fortune, and being invigorated by a chill temperature while the city was still asleep. I'd always liked Ola; his energy was infectious and he always seemed to have a smile on his face. I completely lost track of him after returning to Scotland at the start of 2005, and so when I saw him on TV being interviewed prior to his fight against Enzo Maccarinelli in early 2009, I couldn't have been more surprised. Nobody in the UK knew who he was and most watching the fight had him down as an opponent Enzo would brush aside with ease. But having watched Ola spar countless rounds at Wild Card, I knew he had the skills and guile to upset the odds. I watched the fight with Terry McCormack and a few others at a sports bar in Edinburgh, and must have been the only one there who was rooting for Ola. At stake was the WBO interim cruiserweight title and Ola was only given this shot after Maccarinelli's original opponent pulled out at short notice. Seizing the opportunity, Ola emerged with both the title and the opportunity to go on to better things. He more than deserved the accolades after what had been an excellent performance. Clearly, all the time and effort he'd spent studying James Toney had paid off. Watching him box against Enzo was in fact just like watching a taller and rangier version of Toney.

But even though rooting for Ola, I could not help but feel for Enzo Maccarinelli at the same time. He was still in the process of rebuilding a career that had lost momentum after he went down to a KO by David Haye in the second round of one of the most eagerly anticipated domestic fights in years. That was in March 2008. In December of the same year, he returned with a victory over journeyman heavyweight Mathew Ellis. Now here he was in March 2009, dropping back down to cruiserweight for a crack at the WBO interim title in a fight he'd been expected to win but in which he was beaten, again by KO. It only went to prove that the career of a fighter can be made or destroyed by a single punch. In which other sport or profession is success and failure so precariously balanced?

I drove over to Nigel's old apartment on Beechwood Canyon Drive without knowing if he was still there. I hadn't called beforehand and therefore was a bit unsure about showing up unannounced. I parked in a street that held memories. A female voice answered the intercom. I introduced myself and she buzzed me in, whereupon I made my way along a short passage, through another gate and on past a small swimming pool. Memories of the old days when I used to come over to his place to watch the fights or just spend an hour or two discussing the gym, boxing and life in general returned in abundance.

The blinds were drawn and the apartment was in darkness as I entered. The woman who'd answered the intercom, it turned out, was Nigel's nurse. Though surprised, she seemed pleased to see me. When she told me that he didn't get many visitors, my heart plunged. He was in bed and she went through to wake him and let him know that I was here. A few moments later she returned and told me it was okay to go in. I walked through to the bedroom not knowing what to expect. Nigel smiled when he saw me. I approached the bed and we clasped hands. His condition meant he had difficulty with speech and was prone to regular involuntary shaking fits. I decided not to focus on the negative, though, and we spent the next hour reminiscing about the old days at the gym and the banter we used to have. Soon he was animated, recalling those times with a glint in his eye. Before leaving, I promised to return and see him again before the end of my trip. At the door of his apartment, I asked the nurse about his prognosis. She looked at me and shook her head. His condition was permanent. I walked back to the car with tears in my eyes. Driving away, I cursed the world and everything in it.

22

I CAUGHT up with Andy a couple of days later. We met on the corner of Melrose and Fairfax, just up from where I was staying, and hugged like two brothers being reunited after being parted for a long time. LA is a place where men hug one another as effortlessly as they shake hands elsewhere. We jumped back into our respective cars – a brand new Mercedes-Benz in his case and a cheap and cheerful rental in mine – and off we went, heading for his house in Los Feliz, East LA.

Pulling up outside the place some 20 minutes later, I understood why he'd been so eager to have me over. Prior to me arriving in LA, he'd told me that things had turned around and business was booming. He'd also met a girl and settled down, which in conjunction with the purchase of this house in Los Feliz suggested that, for him at least, the American Dream had come to pass. When I lived here, we'd both been pursuing the same goal of success in Hollywood – in my case as a writer, in his as an actor. But as mentioned, after a few years spent struggling and with no sign of progress, Andy decided to park his acting ambitions and return to his previous career as a broker. I couldn't fault him for that. He was a proud guy, the product of the rougher side of New York, and consequently the constant rejection that an actor endures, allied to the hand-to-mouth existence, was harder for someone like him to accept than most. In truth it cut deep, messed with his self-esteem, which was evident in the way that he always seemed to be angry in those days. I lost count of the number of road rage incidents he was involved in. Nearly every day, he'd call me up and describe how he'd been in a fight or an argument with some guy or other in the street. One particularly memorable afternoon, while facing him across a table over lunch at an eaterie on Beverly Boulevard, he suddenly looked over my shoulder and barked at a guy who was sitting a few tables away.

'Yo man, what's up?!'

It was an eruption of aggression that seemed to come out of nowhere. Later, he explained that the guy in question had been staring at him. So clearly, back then, Andy was in a bad place, struggling to cope with the lack of progress in his acting career and the financial strain that is part and parcel of that life.

One perfect summer's evening, I went out for a spin with him in his Porsche convertible. With the top down, we drove all the way down Sunset to where it ends at Malibu. On the way, Andy told me that in the past he'd made and blown a fortune, most of it partying. Realising he was on a slippery slope, he went sober and turned to religion to help him stay that way, espousing a belief in God that, to his credit, he never tried to force on me when we were together. Back then he was wrestling with a few private demons, I sensed, still trying to escape a past that had come close to destroying him. The result was a man who was not only unhappy but also unhappy about the fact he was unhappy and unable to identify the source of the problem.

When I pointed out the absurdity of the situation – the fact that he was feeling miserable while driving a Porsche convertible through Bel Air all the way down to Malibu along Sunset Boulevard under a star-strewn sky with a warm breeze stroking our faces – he burst out laughing.

I remember imparting on him a nugget of Eastern philosophy I'd picked up and which had always remained with me. To wit: 'The secret to being happy is to be happy.'

I don't think this particular piece of advice resonated or registered to any significant degree.

Anyway, here we were five years on with the fruits of his decision to quit acting to return to his previous career reflected in the large split-level house he'd just moved in to – not forgetting the mint blue Ferrari parked alongside the top-of-the-range BMW in the garage.

After dinner, sitting out on his large balcony drinking tea he'd made and basking in one of those cool LA nights I'd always relished, I detected that for all his material success there was still a gap in Andy's life. As we chatted, he opened up, confessing that he was still drawn to acting, despite failing to make any headway after years spent trying to break into it. The goal of an acting career had brought him out to LA 20 years earlier. The upshot is that regardless of the big house, the fancy cars in the garage and healthy bank account, he still wasn't content. It was an interesting phenomenon to ponder.

Ultimately, there's a difference between living for the approval of others and living for yourself. It reminded me of the ancient Greek exhortation to 'know thyself', and how the difference between knowing who you are and being who you are describes the gulf between the fear of failure and the courage of conviction.

It was a philosophy that applied to boxing. On any given day in gyms all over the world young men – and increasingly women – dedicate themselves to the quest for success in what is arguably the toughest business of all. The vast majority are destined to fail, with all the years spent training, sparring, doing early-morning roadwork and fighting leaving them with just memories and hopefully their health intact to show for it. In most boxing gyms, there's always the guy who once had the promise and potential to go all the way, whose star was in the ascendancy in bygone days. He can boast of having been a local champion, perhaps even a national amateur champion at one time, before embarking on a career in the pros.

But along the way, the wheels came off and his career petered out, almost before it began. Life got in the way in the form of a wife and kids, while promoters failed to come through as promised. By this stage, making peanuts, he was forced to take a job to make ends meet. Before long, his training suffered and he started taking shortcuts – missing runs, cutting his time at the gym, perennially tired and listless. Eventually, and inevitably, he joined the ranks of the journeymen. Rather than the prospect he'd once been, he was now being fed as a human punchbag to a new generation of prospects, his only motivation being to make regular money, with any notion of winning titles and glory receding in importance.

Most fighters are just two or three bad performances away from such a fate, from being relegated to the ranks of those who exist rather than live in the sport. As time passes, the pressure to succeed for a young fighter grows more intense, along with the realisation that there exists a fine line between persistence and delusion. In a town like LA, with its culture of fame fuelled by the belief that dreams can come true, you are reminded of this fine line every minute of every day. The bars, restaurants, coffee shops and hotels are packed with people who arrived determined and committed to achieving their dreams, whether as actors, screenwriters, directors or producers. Many are genuinely talented, some the products of the finest film and acting schools in the business. Yet here they are, years – some even decades – down the road, still struggling to achieve the success they're so desperate to attain.

Most of them become bitter and disenchanted and give up, either settling down to pursue some other career, something more realistic in LA, or returning home to do likewise. The diehards, those who decide to hang on in the hope their fortunes will eventually change and they will at last succeed in their career of choice, end up lost amid the human flotsam that makes up a large part of this city of broken dreams. Only a tiny, tiny few catch that elusive break and are saved from the fate of obscurity that is the lot of the overwhelming majority who embark on this particular and perilous journey.

The similarities between this quest for success in Hollywood and boxing I found striking. The courage required to even decide on a career in boxing is considerable. And even those who don't make it – and, worse still, end up damaged in the attempt – can at least draw comfort from the fact that they dared. This attribute alone sets them on a higher plane from those who never strive, never take chances and never risk anything, while in many cases articulating their scorn for those who do.

I'd purposely timed my 2009 trip to LA to coincide with the arrival of Terry McCormack's group from Lochend to train and spar at Wild Card for a couple of weeks. Terry brought over a few of his most promising amateurs, among them future world champion Josh Taylor, to see how they held up against some of the best in the game. Also in the group was Ken Buchanan, one of Freddie Roach's favourite fighters, with Terry looking forward to introducing them.

In the four days I had left before flying home, I watched the Lochend fighters acquit themselves well in sparring. It would have been understandable if they'd been overawed and wracked with nerves, surrounded as they were by some superb talent – fighters of the calibre of Guillermo Rigondeaux, for example. But instead they rose to the occasion and impressed. I recall watching Josh spar with Rigondeaux, who'd won gold at both the 2000 and 2004 Olympics in the bantamweight division for Cuba.

At this stage of his career, Josh's focus was on making the GB team for the London Olympics, three years down the road, and tests such as this against the highly rated Cuban were crucial to his development. Freddie had only just started training Rigondeaux and big things were expected of him. He certainly carried himself like a champion – confident and self-assured. As Terry put the finishing touches to Josh's headguard in the corner, Rigondeaux stood across the other side of the ring, ready to go with his arms folded, waiting for him to finish and the session to begin. He looked like a man who'd just arrived at the beach, he was so relaxed.

Yet over the three rounds they sparred, Josh, still only a young up-and-coming amateur, gave Rigondeaux something to think about. The Cuban was unable to land a clean shot in the first round; Josh was too fast, moving in and out of range like his feet were on fire. By the middle of the second, confidence growing, he started taking chances, staying in the pocket longer than was clever against a fighter of Rigondeaux's quality. The Cuban proceeded to counter with terrific handspeed of his own, taking command of the centre of the ring. The later, maturer version of Josh Taylor would have reverted back to the tactics of the first round, boxing on the move to avoid being caught needlessly. The Josh Taylor of 2009 was braver than he needed to be, caught up in the occasion, eager to make a statement at the Wild Card Boxing Club, this internationally renowned gym that had taken on the mantle of a crucible in which dreams were dreamt in sweat and blood.

Ultimately, Josh Taylor acquitted himself supremely well against an elite fighter and one of the best he would ever face. Rigondeaux's speed and guile were something to savour and just from those few rounds of sparring, you could tell both fighters were destined for great things.

John Thain sparred a tough Mexican whose name I don't recall. Regardless, he gave John a tough time, which included the liberal employment of low blows. It reached the point where Terry threatened to pull John out after making his anger known to the other corner. To describe the guy he was sparring as rough was an understatement. He was also considerably heavier and experienced in the roughhouse tactics of a seasoned pro. John had still to make his pro debut, yet you wouldn't have thought so the way he threw sharp combinations and moved around the ring with confidence. Halfway through the spar, Pep came over to me and said, 'What's that kid's name?' I told him, to which he replied, 'He's got balls.'

Though, as mentioned, Freddie was in the Philippines with Manny preparing for Pacquiao's upcoming fight against

Miguel Cotto, he was due back in a week or so, which meant Terry and the group would get to see him for a couple of days before returning home. Roach was now boxing's man of the moment. He'd travelled a long way since I first met him in the mid-nineties at the Outlaw Gym. Back then, he typically trained guys fighting at hotel shows and at various other local and lesser venues. Fourteen years on and his services were in demand by a host of world champions and top contenders.

Britain's Amir Khan was one such contender, joining Roach's stable after going down to a brutal KO against Colombia's Breidis Prescott in 2008. Watching him going through a pad workout with one of Freddie's assistants one afternoon at Wild Card, I thought his speed and snap were extraordinary. Questions surrounding his chin hadn't gone away since losing to Prescott, though. But then it was this seeming weakness in conjunction with his undoubted power and speed that made him so exciting to watch. Since decamping from Bolton, England to LA to train under Freddie's tutelage, Khan's career had turned around and again big things were expected. Sparring regularly with Manny Pacquiao and being involved in the gym wars for which Wild Card was renowned looked to have paid off.

Vying for the most memorable moment during those two weeks at Wild Card was the reaction to Ken Buchanan's presence in the gym. The memory of him walking in with Terry and the rest of the group from Lochend and quietly sitting down in one of the chairs against the wall remains vivid. I went over and sat down beside him to watch the action unfold. At one point, the young guy working on the heavy bag adjacent glanced round, noticed Ken and exclaimed, 'Ken Buchanan!' before bounding over to pay his respects. It was the catalyst for others in the gym to do likewise. Within seconds, the Edinburgh lightweight legend found himself mobbed by wellwishers, most of them fighters. Ken, though, appeared more embarrassed than satisfied by all the attention and didn't really know what to say. It was a moving tribute, made more so by its spontaneity, and he deserved nothing less.

SPEAKING OF Amir Khan, Alex Arthur had signed to fight on the undercard of his December 2009 fight in Newcastle against the hitherto undefeated Dmitriy Salita of New York. Alex's scheduled opponent was Nigel Wright, a southpaw from Leeds with a record that suggested he wouldn't present too stern a test. It would be Alex's first outing at light-welterweight and his second outing since losing his super-featherweight title to London's Nicky Cook in 2008. In between, he'd registered a comfortable victory over an outmatched Moroccan, Mohamed Benbiou, in Glasgow. Now it was time to step things up as he set about clawing his way back into contention for a title shot.

By the beginning of December I'd been watching Alex train at Lochend under Terry McCormack's supervision for six or seven months. In that time, he'd worked consistently well and looked good; the experience he'd amassed during a long career evident in the way he was performing while sparring with the gym's stable of younger prospects. When they shared the ring with Alex they upped their game, forcing him to switch on and not rest on his laurels.

I arranged to travel down to Alex's fight with John Thain, who'd been one of his main sparring partners leading up. The opportunity to watch the likes of Kevin Mitchell, James De Gale, Scotland's John Simpson and Enzo Maccarinelli fight on the same card was too good to pass up. With Amir Khan the main event, a quality night of boxing at Newcastle's Metro Arena was guaranteed.

Young John and I made the journey in the beat-up car he was driving at the time. We'd enjoyed a hard running session at Arthur's Seat earlier in the morning and when he arrived to pick me up for the journey down, he was beaming with excitement. The only problem was that the car he arrived in had no reverse gear and was on its last legs. It would be an achievement just getting there and I got in beside him full of trepidation. Despite this, on the way he was excited and animated. As for me, I was sullen and quiet. He obviously noticed because at one point he turned his eyes from the road to ask if I was feeling okay. I brushed him off with a stiff assurance that everything was fine. I was lying. Everything was not fine. On the contrary, it was about as far from fucking fine as it was possible to be. What John didn't know, and what I could never divulge, was that I'd placed a heavy bet on Amir Khan at the bookies the previous night, which comprised near enough every penny I had to my name at the time. Sitting in the car on the way to Newcastle, I wished now I hadn't. Even the young guy behind the counter in the bookies had looked at me askance when I handed over the cash before calling in to get the necessary clearance to accept the bet. Now I was struggling with the consequences of what could well turn out to be the stupidest thing I'd ever done. The thing is I'd never been a betting man – gambling, the bookies, the entire culture had always been alien to me, the fruits of an upbringing spent watching my old man lose on the horses week in and week out. It was Jimmy's fault. An old friend of Terry's, Jimmy was a regular at the gym and something of a local legend. He'd been placing large bets on fights on a regular basis for the past few months and never seemed to lose. At the start of the week he'd walk into Lochend with a wide grin on his face, the result of yet another win at the bookies, and eventually his winning streak rubbed off on me. I wanted some of what he was getting and so when this fight came round, I decided to take the plunge. The result was that instead of looking forward to Newcastle, as I should have been, I was dreading it.

On the way we stopped off at a roadside cafe. We had time to kill, having set off early, and decided to take B roads down rather than the motorway. Getting to Newcastle from Edinburgh by car normally took around two hours. It would take us closer to four. We spent the entire journey talking about boxing, debating the merits of past fighters, dissecting some of the classic fights, and so on. Boxing was John's life; it was all he talked and thought about. His favourite fighters were Alexis Arguello and Tommy Hearns, both tall and rangy like himself. Over lunch we discussed some of the great fights they'd been involved in. I had a particular liking for Hearns, surely one of the most exciting fighters ever to grace the ring. His epic clashes with Leonard, Hagler and Duran still retained an aura of excitement whenever watching or discussing them. In the ring Hearns almost defied nature in that his long, skinny legs and light-boned frame made him an unlikely knockout artist, even though a record of 48 KOs in 67 fights did not lie in this regard. John had spent hours studying his fights, looking for answers to his own dilemma when it came to generating power. Hearns had terrific handspeed and a snap that compensated for his lack of natural body strength and weight. When he threw a right hand it came all the way from the floor, so that by the time his hand left his shoulder the kinetic energy generated as the shot travelled through his body was immense. Watching John on the pads and heavy bag, throwing his own right hands, I often wondered if the problem where he was concerned was more psychological than physical, almost as if he had no confidence in his right hand and so threw it half-heartedly. It was the one weakness in an otherwise excellent package, which if corrected would give him a good chance of challenging for a British title. One thing beyond question where he was concerned was that whatever the potential he possessed, it would be fulfilled. The total dedication, application and commitment with which he pursued his craft made that certain.

While discussing the considerable achievements and merits of Tommy 'The Hitman' Hearns in the unlikely setting of a near-empty roadside restaurant in the middle of nowhere, somewhere on the B road to Newcastle from Edinburgh, I changed the subject to Sugar Ray Leonard's fight against Marvin Hagler in 1987, another all-time classic.

The road to this fight could be traced back to the night Hagler laboured to an 11th-round stoppage against John 'The Beast' Mugabi a year earlier. Seated ringside was Leonard, by this point retired for two years. Watching Hagler struggle to overcome an opponent everyone had expected him to defeat comfortably imbued the former Olympic champion with the belief that he could come back and beat Hagler, even though the bald warrior's reign as world middleweight champion appeared as solid as the foundations of the Great Wall of China. Despite his lacklustre performance against Mugabi, Hagler hadn't lost in 11 years and was considered one of the most fearsome fighters of any era. Making the challenge seem even more unlikely, given Hagler's record and the two years Leonard had spent out of the ring, was the fact that in his last fight before opting to retire for the second time, Ray had been knocked to the canvas by Kevin Howard, a fighter who most would have adjudged to be levels below a prime Leonard. The fight against Howard had been Leonard's first in two years, after retiring for the first time in 1982 with a detached retina. Now here he was proposing to come back for a second time against none other than Marvelous Marvin Hagler.

Hagler's was a ring career built the hard way. In contrast to Leonard, who'd been groomed for stardom throughout his amateur career, which culminated in a gold medal at the 1976 Montreal Olympics, and whose purse for his first pro fight was an unheard-of $40,000, Hagler rose without fanfare before turning pro in 1973, making his debut for a purse of just 50 bucks. Thereafter it took him six years and 46 fights before he got his first title shot against Vito Antuofermo. Even then it seemed the gods were against him, as the contest was inexplicably scored a draw. This was despite the fact that the fight ended with hardly a mark on Hagler's face while Antuofermo's was heavily bruised and swollen. It carried on a pattern that dogged Hagler throughout his career, wherein he believed that he never got the credit or respect he deserved.

Sugar Ray, on the other hand, was boxing's golden boy, the fighter who'd taken on Ali's mantle to become a household name in and out of the ring. Lucrative endorsements, feted by all and sundry, Leonard was to boxing what Elvis had been to music throughout the late seventies and on into the eighties. Yet despite the accolades and riches he garnered in a career consisting of some of the most dazzling performances ever seen in a ring against a host of legendary opponents, he still wasn't satisfied. He felt he needed Hagler on his record to cement his legacy. With Hagler feeling the same way about him, the fight was agreed and set to take place at Caesars Palace in Las Vegas on 6 April 1987. The hype generated in the build-up reflected the stakes that were on the line. The well of resentment within Hagler over Leonard's popularity and status as the darling of the sport ran deep, and he was determined to put things right by knocking him out. In this he had reason to be confident, having KO'd 52 out of 66 opponents and been consistently active, thus maintaining that all-important momentum. His connections felt that Leonard would be no match for Hagler's relentless pressure and intensity, and looked forward to the perfect climax to a remarkable career. They were entitled to believe this, what with Leonard's prolonged inactivity and his underwhelming performance in his last fight two years before against Kevin Howard.

Leonard was under no illusions that he was rolling the dice and he was almost alone in believing that he could defeat Hagler. As part of his preparations he tested himself in a couple of real fights behind closed doors – complete with regulation gloves, referee, and no headgear – in an effort to get rid of the inevitable ring rust that he'd accrued due to such a long period of inactivity. In terms of his gameplan for Hagler, he only decided that he would box and move the week before the fight. His original plan had been to go toe to toe and trade, but this approach was abandoned after he almost got knocked out by one of his sparring partners. Leonard and his trainer Angelo Dundee's decision to change the gameplan accordingly would prove crucial to the outcome.

Ray entered the ring wearing a robe that was straight out of the wardrobe department of the popular eighties US soap series *Dynasty*, complete with shoulder pads. He looked more like the rock star Prince than a man who'd participated in some of the most enthralling fights of any era in the sport of boxing. He looked relaxed and confident as Hagler's brooding presence across the other side of the ring left no doubt that he'd prepared like a man intent on removing and bagging his opponent's organs one by one. In the unlikely setting of an outdoor arena in the parking lot of an establishment that the Emperor Caligula would have considered vulgar, time was about to be hurled back to when a man ate what he could kill. Nature's laws, not man's, would decide this event, involving a suspension of civilisation and modernity for however long it took.

From the opening bell the template was set. Hagler would be the aggressor while Leonard would box on the back foot, try to make him miss and then counter. It was Leonard's strategy which proved the more effective in the early rounds, during which Hagler struggled to get to grips with his opponent's movement and handspeed. Time after time, Hagler trapped Leonard against the ropes only for Leonard to explode into a flurry of short punches that dazzled the crowd and impressed the judges. In the process, he built a strong lead but in the fifth round started to tire and slow down, allowing Hagler to land clean for the first time. As the round neared its end, Leonard looked in trouble as his opponent piled on the pressure. But inspired by a partisan crowd, the former Olympic champion dug deep and survived. On his stool before coming out for the sixth, he somehow managed to dredge up the will and stamina to dance and move as if it was the first, causing Hagler to revert back to following him around the ring trying to close the distance and growing frustrated at his inability to do so. At times it was as if Leonard had him on a leash, leading him around the ring while keeping out of range. It was an example of ring generalship rarely equalled.

The judges' split decision at the end went Leonard's way and has been a topic of debate ever since. Some feel Hagler should have won because he was the aggressor and connected with the harder and more effective punches. Those on the other side of the argument, this writer included, counter with the argument that Leonard connected with more of his punches and was able to make Hagler miss with most of his. Leonard was quicker to the punch throughout and there's a difference between pressure and 'effective' pressure, with Hagler's performance on the night more redolent of the former than the latter. Regardless of the controversy, it was a classic contest between contrasting styles, boxer versus fighter, with the boxer on this occasion emerging victorious.

Marvelous Marvin Hagler remained bitter about the decision ever after. He never fought again and turned his back on the sport over the next few years. However, despite the loss, his status as a legend has never been in doubt. Sugar Ray went on to fight a further five times, finally retiring in 1997 after losing to Hector Camacho in his second defeat on the bounce. It was a sad end to a glittering career. Regardless, as with Marvin Hagler, his legacy was and remains secure.

By the time we re-emerged from the roadside cafe, John and I were eager to get to Newcastle. The fact that his car had no reverse gear momentarily slipped John's mind when he parked head in against a wall upon our arrival. It meant we had to push the car out of its parking space before we could set off. It occurred to me that Sugar Ray Leonard and Marvelous Marvin Hagler wouldn't have to do this. John laughed when I shared the thought. I would have been happy to join him if not for the fact I still had a few hours to wait before learning if my decision to place a large bet on Amir Khan was the stupidest thing I'd ever done.

After a short spell spent driving around the centre of Newcastle looking for the hotel where Alex Arthur, Terry and Terry's assistant, John McCarron, were staying, and where they'd told us to meet them when we arrived, we finally pulled up outside. It was located on the Quayside, which like most waterfront districts in cities the length and breadth of Britain had been gentrified in the wake of the nation's deindustrialisation. Upmarket hotels, restaurants, bars and other attractions had replaced the huge cranes, ships and shipping containers of yesteryear. I can't recall the name of the hotel now but it was a big place and offered the kind of comfort that professional fighters deserve. It turned out that most of the fighters and their teams were staying here, as well as most of the press who'd descended on the city to cover the event. I made my way in and up to the room being shared by Terry and John McCarron, while John parked in the adjoining hotel parking garage.

Terry was just about to go up to Alex's room to check on him before they headed over to the venue, when I joined them. Alex's fight was one of the first on the undercard, which was unknown territory for someone used to headlining shows. I wondered how he would handle this relative decline in status as he set about the process of rebuilding after a couple of setbacks. I asked Terry if he'd had the opportunity to meet up with Freddie Roach, who was staying at another hotel nearby with Amir Khan and his team. Terry told me he'd seen him briefly the previous night. I was keen to find out how Khan was looking, seeking reassurance with my bet in mind, and was relieved to find out that, according to Freddie, he was in good shape. No matter, I was still keeping the bet to myself and almost giving myself an ulcer in the process.

Young John joined us and we all headed up to Alex's room on the next floor. We found him lying on his bed watching TV. He seemed in good form and completely unfazed over the fact that he had a fight coming up in just a couple of hours' time. But then he was used to this by now. He'd fought all over the world and was an old hand at the game. Why should he worry about facing an opponent whom most felt he would overcome with relative ease?

I couldn't help noticing the remnants of a meal on the tray by Alex's bedside. The prevailing wisdom in boxing that after the weigh-in a fighter should eat to put on weight prior to stepping into the ring, normally the day after, was fundamentally flawed in my view. Eat too much and you overload your digestive system, with the result that you climb into the ring feeling sluggish. Some fighters have been known to put on as much as 15 pounds between the weigh-in and the fight. This thinking was based on the myth that a fighter's weight determines the power behind his shots.

Anyway, it came time to go and outside the hotel we all piled into one of the shuttle vans that the show's promoter, Frank Warren, had provided to ferry the fighters and their teams to the venue. It was an impressive-looking arena and as the van pulled up outside the fighters' and officials' entrance at the rear of the building, the sense of anticipation began to build. John Thain and I were able to squeeze in backstage as part of Alex's team. Seeing the ring in the middle of this considerable arena, albeit still empty, induced a rush of adrenalin. I could only imagine what it must be like for the fighters. The sense of occasion – the realisation that months of early-morning roadwork, sparring, dieting and dedication was about to be put on the line – would surely be enormous.

Alex was sharing his changing room with James DeGale and Enzo Maccarinelli, among others. We were first to arrive and without wasting time preparations began; Alex getting changed into his warm-up gear, while Terry and John McCarron began removing everything required to get him ready from a large training bag – gloves, handwraps, Vaseline, water and so on. I sat on the bench and watched it unfold, impressed by their focus and professionalism. As head trainer, Terry in particular was under a lot of pressure, especially with the fight being covered on television and with the advent of microphones in the corner between rounds picking up the exchanges between trainer and fighter. At this point in the sport's history, trainers were scrutinised, talked about and either lauded or criticised almost as much as the fighters.

Other fighters and their teams began to arrive while all this was going on and the dressing room soon filled up. Alex knew most of them – fellow fighters – and the banter was not long in starting up. James DeGale preferred to keep himself to himself. He was the new golden boy of British boxing, riding high after winning a gold medal at the Beijing Olympics. He'd only had five or six pro fights and big things were expected. His style was flashy but effective, very slick with fast hands, and I was looking forward to following his progress.

Big Enzo arrived sporting a grin that was a mile wide. He had a warm handshake and a greeting for everyone. You'd never have thought he was in the process of rebuilding his career following back-to-back losses, one of those the devastating KO by Ola Afolabi we've already discussed. At his peak, Maccarinelli was part of Enzo Calzaghe's famed Newbridge Gym stable, along with Joe Calzaghe, Nathan Cleverly and Gavin Rees, and was considered one of the most exciting fighters in the country. He could punch with the best of them and when he met David Haye in their much-anticipated cruiserweight unification clash in March 2008, he seemed on the cusp of big things. Destined to be a short fight between two guys who could bang, and who had proved in past fights they had a suspect chin, it was always going to come down to who connected first. It turned out to be Haye, who caught Enzo with a right hand in the second round and went on to bludgeon him against the ropes until the referee stepped in to stop it. Haye went on to establish himself as a major force at heavyweight, winning a world title and headlining stadium fights, while Enzo's career travelled in the opposite direction. I studied him as he floated around the room, exuding the kind of charm and gregariousness you wouldn't associate with a man about to step into a boxing ring. I wondered if his relaxed demeanour was a façade or was indeed authentic. His stock had plummeted and it was reflected in the fact he was on tonight's bill as a 'floater'. This meant he would be on between bouts to fill any gaps in the TV schedule that might appear as a result of an early stoppage or KO. He could be fighting early or late, depending on what happened with the main events. You would think being a floater might be an ignominious position for a former world champion to be in, yet watching him you wouldn't have known it.

Pretty soon the changing room was alive with the energy of fighters warming up and getting ready. Terry took Alex into an adjacent space to get him warmed up on the mitts. I stood watching him throw crisp combinations, which just as when I'd watched Brad warming up for his fight in the States all the way back in 1995, echoed like gunshots in the enclosed space.

Over the next couple of hours, fighter after fighter left the changing room for the ring before returning later in a state of barely disguised relief and euphoria if they'd won, or crushing disappointment if they'd lost. The entire gamut of human emotions was on display, which should not have come as a surprise given that if the ring is where a boxer comes face to face with his opponent, the changing room is where he struggles with his demons. I was moved to write something about it afterwards.

Prior to the fight, usually between one and two hours before, the fighter enters the changing room with his team. Unless he's the main event, he'll be sharing the changing room with three or four other fighters appearing on the same bill. Each camp stakes their territory in a different corner, where the respective trainers begin unpacking the tape and gauze, Vaseline and other assorted items they need to get their fighter prepared. The easy, relaxed banter that passes between the various camps, between fighters who in most cases already know one another from so many nights like this, belies a tension that comes with the knowledge of the physical and mental test to come.

Each fighter runs the same questions over and over inside his head: *'Am I ready? Have I trained hard enough? Have I done enough roadwork? Did I get the right sparring? Am I over that last defeat? Do I still have what it takes? Can I really beat this guy?'*

These are private questions he asks of himself, all the while smiling and appearing relaxed in a studied effort

218

at maintaining the aura of confidence he's perfected over time.

As the time moves perilously closer to the fight, most fighters find it impossible to sit still. They walk up and down, many of them playing around with an iPod, periodically exploding into a short burst of shadowboxing in front of the mirror on the wall on the back of a surge of nervous energy. In every changing room at every boxing show a boombox is obligatory, the music changing constantly according to the different tastes of the various fighters there.

With half an hour to go, it's time to start wrapping the fighter's hands. This the trainer does with the concentration of a surgeon performing a lifesaving operation. There's an intimacy between the fighter and his trainer now, a trust born of the fact that the trainer, more than any other person in the fighter's life, knows his strengths and weaknesses, which to any fighter is akin to the possession of a state secret.

During this time, various officials appear. One arrives with a clipboard and pen requesting the names of the fighter's trainer and cornermen; another asks to see the shorts the fighter will be wearing to make sure the colours don't clash with those of his opponent in the interests of the television broadcaster.

In comes the referee. He introduces himself before going through his pre-fight instructions. 'No holding. When I tell you to break, I expect you to do so immediately. No punching on the back of the head. If you go to the body, keep your punches above the waist. Obey my commands at all times. Good luck and God bless.'

The referee leaves and now it's time for the cutsman to apply Vaseline around the fighter's eyes, nose and across his cheeks. Hands duly wrapped, the fighter removes his tracksuit and puts on first his protective cup, then his shorts, followed by his gloves.

The culmination of months of cold, lonely mornings pounding the streets to get the lungs in shape has arrived, not forgetting the hard sessions in the gym consisting of dozens of rounds of sparring, pad work, endless rounds on the bags, floor work, strength and conditioning; weeks spent dieting, sacrificing nights out with friends, denying himself the comforts and pleasures of a normal existence – all for this one night.

As soon as the gloves are tied and taped, he starts warming up, beginning with some perfunctory stretching, then a minute or so of shadowboxing to get the arms loose before his trainer slips on a set of mitts and the fighter starts throwing combinations, the sound of his punches, crisp and sharp, comforting him with a magnified sense of power. Periodically, members of his team leave the room and arrive back with an update on the progress of the preceding fight.

Finally, with tension near breaking point, the door opens to reveal another official. 'Thirty seconds!' he barks.

The fighter removes his t-shirt and gets into his robe. A last drink of water is administered by one of his team, while his trainer gives him instructions. 'Keep him at the end of your jab. Remember, he's open to the right uppercut. Watch that left hook and keep your feet moving. He's not in your league, this guy. Come on, let's do this. Let's go.'

It's time and out he goes with his team following behind, acknowledging the words of encouragement from others in the changing room in the process.

As soon as the fighter leaves for the ring, the door closes behind him and a fleeting, morbid silence descends among those he's left behind. It briefly rips the mask from the masquerade of nonchalance to reveal anxiety and nerves. Outside the womb-like sanctuary of the changing room lies the unforgiving and hostile attention of television cameras, the crowd and an opponent every bit as desperate and determined to win as they are. At stake is more than pride. At stake is the fighter's future, his family's future, his dream of attaining the title and financial security that comes with it.

Thankfully, the banter resumes after a few seconds, banishing both the silence and muted noise of the crowd on the other side of the door.

In no time at all, it seems, the fighter who just left for the ring returns with his team.

If he's victorious, the energy level is sent rocketing with euphoria as he basks in the congratulations of all and sundry, including family members who join him to share in his triumph. His spouse or girlfriend peppers him with kisses, crying tears of both joy and grief at the sight of his bruised, swollen features. Overriding every other emotion, though, is relief. At last, they can relax and look forward to a few weeks of normal life doing the things that other couples do and take for granted. Soon after, his manager or promoter appears with talk of bigger fights and decent paydays, precisely what the fighter wants to hear as he gets ready to go and celebrate his win.

If, on the other hand, he returns to the changing room defeated, the gloom he brings with him is an unwelcome intrusion. His face bruised, shorts and boots spattered with specks of dried blood, he engages in a futile attempt to keep up a brave face, smiling as he begins the process of explaining himself, the reasons for the defeat and his performance to family, friends and everyone he meets.

The truth is that inside he's crumbling with despair and humiliation and all he wants is to be alone. On his mind is the future. *'Is this the end? Will I be able to get another fight? Will the promoter renew my contract? Do I have enough money put by just in case?'*

As this emotional rollercoaster continues, in another corner of the room another fighter starts to get ready.

24

ALEX ARTHUR lost.

He'd appeared out of sorts from the opening bell against Nigel Wright, and it was painful to watch. On his way to the ring he couldn't have failed to notice the smattering of spectators in the arena this early in proceedings. The emptiness was all-encompassing. For a fighter who'd spent most of his career, from the amateurs into the professional ranks, being lauded as a major talent, it must have been hard to reckon with. During the fight he didn't appear comfortable with the move up in weight. It was his first outing at light-welter and it told in the way his opponent was able to soak up his shots, spoil and break up his rhythm. He lost an eight-round decision and when he got back to the changing room afterwards, joined there by his family, I felt for him. When, later, it came to light that he'd been suffering with a blood disorder from as far back as his fight against Nicky Cook, a disorder that drained his strength, his lacklustre performance made sense. He was not a man to court sympathy, though, and despite the loss he still emitted the aura of a champion. There was nothing to be said. The process of analysing and absorbing the defeat would take its course. Ninety-nine per cent of fighters, no matter how successful or accomplished, experience defeat. It's how they come back from it that counts. This, of course, is easier said or written than done. For a man as proud as Alex Arthur, the pain of losing would undoubtedly hurt more than it would most. But on the other hand, his determination to overcome it also burned more fiercely. Boxing was a sport defined by both of these extremes.

Alex would be more than okay, though, going on to establish a successful second career as a boxing pundit and gym owner.

By the time of Amir Khan's fight, the arena was packed and his introduction by the ring announcer met with a wall of noise. This was being mooted as Khan's last fight in the UK for the foreseeable future as he and his team had America in their sights. I was standing off to the side backstage as he started his ring walk. It came after the obligatory pyrotechnics and light show had whipped the crowd into a frenzy. Dimitry Salita, Khan's opponent, was undefeated. Even though his record comprised a questionable calibre of opposition, a perfect record in boxing is not to be sniffed at. As Khan climbed into the ring to receive the acclaim of the crowd, my heart was beating fast with anticipation and dread in equal measure, my mind now completely on my bet.

Thankfully, the gods were with me and within seconds of the opening bell I was jumping on John Thain's back and punching the air after Khan put Salita down with his first flurry of punches. The fight was stopped less than a minute later and relief flooded my veins. John still had no idea about the hefty bet I'd placed on Khan to win, and the expression on his face as I danced around him celebrating suggested he was thinking that I'd lost my mind. As soon as I told him, he laughed. All of a sudden I was the happiest man not just in the Metro Arena but in the whole of Newcastle.

Apart from Alex's loss, it was a great night. The pulsating atmosphere that filled the arena described a card of excellent fights. The stand-out performance for me was Kevin Mitchell's victory over Colombia's Breidis Prescott, the only man to defeat Amir Khan up to this point, which he did in dramatic fashion in 2008 with a brutal first-round KO. As Mitchell squared off against the Colombian in the centre of the ring to receive the ritual pre-fight instructions from the referee, I feared for him. Prescott looked significantly bigger and more powerful and with the emphatic manner of his KO victory over Khan vivid in my mind, I shuddered at the prospect of Mitchell's demise. Prescott was a wrecking machine and I was convinced that the Colombian would blow him away.

But Kevin Mitchell was a fighter with the pride and defiance of London's East End in his blood. More importantly, he'd come to the ring with a gameplan devised by a man in his corner, Jimmy Tibbs, who'd seen it all in boxing and was considered one of the most knowledgeable trainers in the game.

Watching a fight on television is nothing like being at ringside. It's only then you gain an understanding of the physical ordeal fighters endure as they trade punches wearing eight or 10oz gloves. The thud and crack as the punches connect, the concentration etched on their faces as they try to outfox, set traps and read one another is such an intense experience it can leave you emotionally drained just watching it. Watching Kevin Mitchell elude, slip and roll under Prescott's punches was like watching a man dodging bullets. The height and size difference between them was considerable, almost to the point that it seemed doubtful that they'd weighed in on the same scales. Like most watching, I sat there in a state of suspense and dread combined, waiting for one of Prescott's bombs to find the target and leave the Londoner sparked out on the canvas.

But by the middle rounds, Mitchell's dogged and disciplined gameplan of staying out of his opponent's reach was bearing fruit. Prescott was starting to gas and frustration was setting in. Sensing his moment, Mitchell started to unload with effective counters as the crowd roared him on. My heart was in my mouth as the fight approached its climax. When it ended after 12 gripping rounds, the roof almost left the arena such was the crescendo of noise that greeted the final bell.

Kevin Mitchell had put on a masterclass of tactical boxing and deservedly took the decision.

Back at the hotel later the bar was stowed out with fighters, trainers, managers, reporters and shameless hangers-on like me. It was time to relax. The long weeks and months of early-morning roadwork, tough sparring sessions and diet were over and there was a palpable and cathartic sense of release around the place. Terry, John McCarron, John Thain and I joined Terry's partner Jackie and some friends at a table near the back. I was in a good mood. My bet had come up trumps and every time I thought about it a fresh surge of relief washed through my system. By midnight, I was toasted.

After a fitful night's sleep on the floor of Terry and John McCarron's room, we were up early the next morning for a large breakfast. People arrived in the restaurant in dribs and drabs, sporting the evidence of the raucous antics of the previous night in the form of tired eyes and hangdog expressions. On the drive back to Edinburgh, John and I spent a lot of time picking over the previous night's drama, comparing the merits and demerits of each fighter and their performances. John was about to embark on his own career in the pros, set to make his debut in just a few months' time. He had a long, unpredictable and tough road ahead.

When we worked together on his strength and conditioning, I emphasised the need for aggression when it came to executing the explosive part of the movement in the various exercises I had him doing. I often saw fighters training with heavy weights in an attempt to increase their strength, moving the weight slowly through the range of motion. But there's a marked and crucial difference between training for strength and training to develop explosive strength. Fighters need the explosive kind, which is why moving any muscle or muscle group involved in a given exercise slowly through the movement's range of motion is not the kind of strength and conditioning work they should be doing. The concept of muscle memory dictates that the slower a fighter's muscles move in training, the slower they will move in the ring.

For any strength and conditioning programme to be effective in a fighter's preparations, it must be tailored to meet the specific demands of the ring. Anything else is not only a waste of time, it's counterproductive. During my time at Wild Card, Justin Fortune had been Freddie's strength and conditioning coach. Up to then, Freddie never had anyone in that role in his set-up. We're talking here about the early 2000s, when strength and conditioning was just beginning to emerge as a key component of a fighter's training. After Justin and Freddie parted company, Freddie hired Alex Ariza to replace him. Soon, Ariza became nearly as prominent as Freddie in Manny's camp, prior to Freddie firing him before Manny's November 2013 clash against Brandon Rios, whose own trainer, Mickey Garcia, promptly hired Ariza to work with him.

In time, though, I would start to grow cynical about the trend and fixation on strength and conditioning within boxing. Some fighters, it seemed to me, made the mistake of viewing it not merely as an adjunct to their boxing, but almost on a par in order of importance. The danger is that, taken to extremes, a fighter may start to think like a bodybuilder and/or strength athlete rather than an athlete involved in what will always be a sport of skill rather than biceps. While strength and conditioning has an important part to play in a boxer's preparations, it has to be viewed as a means to the end, never the end in itself.

I encountered this problem briefly while working with John. After a couple of months, the results of his new strength and conditioning regimen had manifested in the lean muscle he'd begun to develop. It corresponded with a sharp improvement in his strength, especially on movements such as squats, cleans and bench press. The downside to this was that, psychologically, because of these improvements, he began to make the mistake of thinking he could now go into the ring and trade toe to toe. Terry had to take him aside to remind him that his strength lay in his boxing ability and to focus on that rather than on trying to be a puncher. It's in the womb not the gym that punchers are made, and anyone claiming otherwise is to my mind peddling snake oil. Yes, working on strength and technique will increase power, but not to the extent of turning a fighter with limited power in his shots into one with knockout power.

My role with John was of course marginal. It was the graft he was putting in with Terry every day that was primarily responsible for his development. With his pro debut coming up, Terry was putting him through intense sessions on the pads, correcting his technique, making him dig deep to find reserves of tenacity he probably never even realised he possessed, as he got him ready. This was combined with hard sparring sessions. Whatever happened when he stepped through the ropes for his pro debut, his preparation couldn't have been better.

AT LOCHEND, Paul Appleby was now a regular fixture upon returning to the gym after a brief lay-off to resume his partnership with Terry, who'd trained him when he first turned pro at 19. Paul had enjoyed a near-meteoric rise in the featherweight division thereafter. In 2008 he won the British title against Glasgow's John Simpson in an epic contest that went the distance. Not long after that, he was voted the Best Young Boxer of the Year by the Boxing Writers' Club. It appeared inevitable that he would go on to bigger and better things, especially given the positive media profile he enjoyed, which was driven by a combination of his boyish features and cocky swagger. In the ring his aggressive style had seen him stop most of his opponents, mostly with a trademark left uppercut to the body.

But after winning the title, Appleby's career stalled. He lost focus and discipline, which despite changing trainers he found hard to recapture as he went in against Belfast's Martin Lindsay and lost his title. For the next year or so he drifted before deciding to make a comeback, which is how he came to be reunited with Terry at Lochend.

One thing that stood out about Paul was his appetite for sparring. He loved nothing more than having a tear-up in the ring. It must have been around mid-2010 when he sparred with Ricky Burns. Ricky was travelling through from Glasgow with his trainer Billy Nelson and John Simpson, who at the time was also being trained by Nelson and who, it had been planned, was also going to do a few rounds with Paul. Billy had arranged it with Terry that they would come to Edinburgh the first week for sparring, with Terry and Paul returning the favour with a trip to Glasgow to spar with Ricky and John again at Billy's gym the following week.

There was a buzz about the place when they arrived. Ricky was getting ready to challenge Roman 'Rocky' Martinez for his super featherweight title, while it would be the first time that Paul and John Simpson had shared a ring since their British featherweight title clash two years earlier. Despite being rivals, there was no bad blood between them. The respect they shared was, on the contrary, testament to a sport that to the uninitiated involves two men trying to punch one another's lights out, but which in truth sees courage, skill and determination sit side by side with mutual respect and solidarity, based on the pain and sacrifice all fighters endure.

By the time Paul and Ricky were ready to start the gym was busy, many having turned up specially to watch them spar.

The resulting anticipation was thick as the buzzer sounded and off they went.

Ricky started quickly, setting a ferocious pace as he came forward throwing fast combinations. His intensity took Paul by surprise and he struggled to adjust. It had been a long time since I'd seen anything like the ferocity of Burns' work. This was no pitter-patter sparring session; it was a war, reminding me of the gym wars I used to see on a daily basis at Wild Card back in the day. Paul did the only thing he could do in the circumstances; he dug deep and kept working. He took some heavy shots but refused to succumb. On a couple of occasions, he succeeded in forcing Ricky back against the ropes, but mostly it was all he could do to keep from being overwhelmed.

The three rounds he then did with John Simpson immediately after his four with Ricky were hard going. But with a fighter's heart beating inside his chest, he ground them out.

By the end of proceedings, it was evident that Paul still had work to do to get himself fit and strong enough to compete with the likes of Ricky Burns and John Simpson at this stage of his career. Terry asked me to work with him on his conditioning, and so we did a few sessions together, during which he always gave his all, even though I'm not sure that he particularly enjoyed them.

It was on a brutal winter's night in early December 2010, one of the worst winter's Britain's every experienced, that I travelled through to watch Paul's fight against Joseph

Laryea at the Braehead Arena in Glasgow with Stevie Laidlaw, Billy Doc, and Paul Gray from the gym. They picked me up outside Saughton Prison, and by the time they did my nuts were so cold I was seriously pondering the possibility of breaking into the jail behind me for a bit of warmth.

Thick snow on the ground had me worried about the drive along the M8. Stevie Laidlaw was driving, and by profession was a driving instructor, but nonetheless it was a night when even Scott of the Antarctic would have struggled to get from Edinburgh to Glasgow.

Fortunately, we made it in one piece and, parking, wasted no time in heading into the venue. In the bar there were more scars than you'll find at your average slaughterhouse. None of us spoke the local lingo, 'weegie', and so it was a case of keeping our mouths shut and heads down lest we lose them.

At stake in this fight for Paul was the WBO Intercontinental super featherweight title. His fight against Laryea, a tough Ghanaian, was on the undercard of Ricky Burns' defence of his super featherweight world title against Andreas Evensen. Paul had injured his right hand in his previous fight and subsequently had hurt it again while training for this one. But he was determined to take the Laryea fight and had assured Terry that his hand was fine. Either he'd told Terry this knowing that it wasn't fine, or he hurt it again early in the fight. Whatever it was, the result was a brutal contest during which he found himself on the receiving end of a merciless mauling from his significantly taller and larger opponent for much of it.

It was a night I will never forget for Paul's extraordinary courage and tenacity in staying in there and refusing to quit, despite fighting with one hand. Amazingly, towards the end, he even came back and started turning the tables.

But it was too little too late, with the African emerging the victor by split decision. When Norman Mailer wrote about fighters entering the 'boiler room of the damned' in the ring, he was obviously writing with Paul Appleby in mind.

Making the defeat worse was the fact that Frank Warren, both his and Ricky Burns' promoter at the time, was looking at getting the two of them in the ring early the following year for a domestic showdown that would definitely have drawn a capacity crowd and a lot of interest.

The outcome was further proof that this boxing game could be cruel. To witness a fighter, battered and bruised, leave the ring with a towel over his shoulders after being beaten and beat-up in front of an arena full of people, not to mention the many thousands – in some cases hundreds of thousands – watching at home, reminds you of the truism that 'success has a thousand fathers but failure is an orphan'.

26

WHEN IT comes to this hurt business, otherwise known as prizefighting, a sport that exemplifies both cruelty and magnificence in equal part, Muhammad Ali and Joe Frazier, who in their day formed the fiercest rivalry in the history not only of boxing but conceivably all of sports, are never far from my thoughts. Down through the years I must have watched more footage of them – comprising documentaries, fights and interviews – than all other fighters combined. As with most people who develop an interest in boxing, Ali's name had always loomed largest in my mind. His sublime skills in the ring were enhanced by his courage and principles outside it, epitomised when he refused to be inducted for the war in Vietnam. His defiance against the might of the US military, the courts and political and media establishments has never been equalled by any athlete or sports star since – and most likely never will. Ali stood for something more than self and was willing to sacrifice money and his career in the process, which has fittingly seen him accorded legendary status throughout the world, not just as one of the greatest heavyweights who ever lived but as a great man.

To truly understand Ali, you have to understand the social context of the time and place of which he was a product. It was a period in America's history when blacks still suffered segregation and state-sanctioned racial discrimination in the South. Left in no doubt of their inferior status, their collective self-esteem and racial pride were virtually non-existent.

Ali lived through the tempestuous years of the civil rights movement, the rise of black nationalism and the social and political convulsions that resulted from both. He stood tall and proud at a time when his people were still cowed and the wonder is that he never joined either Martin Luther King or Malcolm X in being assassinated for the stance he took. It might be hard to imagine now but at one time Ali was the most hated man in America; the *bête noire* of a sporting and political establishment that did its best to ensure he was destroyed in return for his refusal to be drafted for the war in Vietnam. His stand shocked the nation, especially as it took place in 1966, when the war was still in its infancy and enjoyed broad public support. Ali's draft status had been reclassified 1-A, which meant he was eligible to serve. Up to then, he'd been deemed ineligible for the draft due to poor test results. His famous quote to the press, 'I ain't got no quarrel with them Vietcong,' resounded like a thunderbolt across the world. It was delivered spontaneously after he spent hours being badgered by reporters for a response to being reclassified. Those same reporters, along with America's leading sportswriters, lined up to attack Ali in the days and weeks following, their vitriol and condemnation dominating both the front and back pages of every newspaper in the country. It was notable that some were unwilling to acknowledge or respect the fact that Ali had changed his name two years previously and was no longer called Cassius Clay. A sample of the contempt for Ali that appeared in the pages of both the local and national print media makes stark reading, even today:

'Squealing over the possibility that the military may call him up, Cassius makes himself as sorry a spectacle as those unwashed punks who picket and demonstrate against the war.'

'As a fighter, Cassius is good. As a man, he cannot compare to some of the kids slogging through the rice paddies where the names are stranger than Muhammad Ali.'

'For his stomach-turning performance, boxing should throw Clay out on his inflated head.'

As a result of his stance on Vietnam, calls to end Ali's boxing career grew to a crescendo. Largely at the behest of a campaign orchestrated by the *Chicago Tribune* newspaper, the Illinois State Athletic Commission decided to revisit its sanctioning of Ali's scheduled fight against Ernie Terrell in Chicago. The fight's promoters, attempting to salvage the bout, arranged for Ali to appear before the state's commission to apologise for his remarks. They were in for a surprise, though, when Ali used the opportunity to reaffirm his right to his own opinion. 'I don't have to apologise,' he said. 'I'm not in court.'

The same day, the Illinois State Attorney announced that it had cancelled the Ali–Terrell bout on the grounds that it violated state law. In desperation the promoters tried to find another venue, only to discover that a domino effect had been unleashed. In short order Louisville, Miami, Pittsburgh and half a dozen other cities were considered before political pressure vetoed it. Meanwhile, in the media the attacks on Ali continued. Arthur Daley, in the *New York Times*, wrote, 'Clay could have been the most popular of all champions. But he attached himself to a hate organization (Nation of Islam) and antagonized everyone with his boasting and his disdain for even a low-grade patriotism.'

Former champion Billy Conn said, 'I'll never go to another one of his fights. He is a disgrace to the boxing profession. And I think that any American who pays to see him fight after what he has said should be ashamed.'

Ali suffered this level of public opprobrium all the way through until April 1967, when he was called to be formally inducted into the US armed forces. Amid a media scrum, he duly arrived at the United States Armed Forces Examining and Entrance Station in Houston to be processed. One of

26 men scheduled to be inducted that morning, he was the only one who refused to take the step forward when called. It was a seminal moment not only in Ali's life but in the social history of the United States, its impact felt by the black liberation and civil rights movements, the burgeoning anti-Vietnam war movement, and all over the world among a new generation of activists determined to bring about social change. An hour after Ali refused to be inducted, the New York State Athletic Commission suspended his boxing licence. Every other state athletic commission did likewise and Ali was stripped of his title. He now faced prison and financial ruin, and his passport was confiscated to ensure he wouldn't be able to make a living outside the country.

Yet over the three years of his exile from the ring, he grew in stature. Speaking at colleges throughout the country, he resonated with young people of every race and background as a man of deep conviction. His defiance in the face of such massive odds inspired others to follow his example.

As a fighter, when he first arrived on the stage of heavyweight boxing in the early 1960s, he did so as something new, a transitional fighter who took the sport in a different direction. Prior to him, heavyweights had typically been flat-footed, slow-handed men who bludgeoned their way through fights with heavy, ponderous punches, wherein the ability to take a punch was as important as the ability to deliver one. Ali's style was so out of the ordinary for a fighter his size, he was written off by most boxing writers of the period when he appeared for the first time on a major stage at the 1960 Rome Olympics. Despite taking gold in the light-heavyweight division, none of them felt he had enough power to succeed as a pro. He moved too much, they felt, wasting energy that would result in him running out of steam and getting tagged. Ali offended their conservative sensibilities when it came to the noble art. A boxing ring was no place for flamboyance. It was an arena in which those white protestant virtues of honest endeavour and tenacity – the very virtues that had built the country – were affirmed. Worse even than flamboyance and braggadocio in a fighter were flamboyance and braggadocio in a black fighter.

In Muhammad Ali, they encountered both in abundance.

On that historic night in Miami in 1964, as we've already touched upon, he answered his detractors by defeating Sonny Liston to win the heavyweight title. Ali, at just 22, nullified Liston's considerable power with his inordinate reflexes, movement and speed. Flying in the face of conventional wisdom, he held his hands low and used his head as bait to draw an opponent's punches, pulling back to make them miss with just millimetres to spare before delivering stinging counters, all the while disorientating and frustrating them with blinding footwork. He was fast, he was tall and he brought poetry to this most primitive of sports.

He also possessed an instinct for self-promotion that was ahead of its time. Before long, his was a household name not only in America but also across the world as he regaled sportswriters with a constant stream of kitsch poetry, fight predictions and a unique ability to ridicule his opponents.

The staid sport of boxing had never seen anything like it; neither had a country in which black sportsmen had become accustomed to behaving in a manner designed to ingratiate them with white America – non-threatening and passive.

After enduring his three-and-a-half-year exile from the ring over his stance when it came to the war in Vietnam, Ali returned in 1970 against Jerry Quarry. Quarry was a top contender and in deciding to face him in his first fight back, Ali was throwing himself in at the deep end.

The former world heavyweight champion's years of inactivity were immediately apparent when he de-robed to reveal an ample girth. They were confirmed after the opening bell with footwork that was markedly slower and timing that was off kilter. This was not the Ali who'd once devastated opponents with blinding speed and uncanny reflexes. That lithe, gangling freak of nature now appeared mortal. He still possessed a lightning whip jab, however, and though no longer able to step away from trouble, he compensated by tying his opponent up in clinches. The fight was stopped at the end of the third due to a cut above Quarry's eye, but it was a result that flattered Ali. The truth could not be denied. He was not the same fighter.

A style that involved holding his chin high and his right hand down by his waist, combined with a tendency to move back in straight lines, especially when he was tired, meant that Ali had always been susceptible to a left hook. During the first half of his career, both Sonny Banks and Henry Cooper had floored him with this particular punch, doing so at a time when his ability to dance and move meant that most of his opponents struggled to lay a glove on him. Now, having slowed down, he was even more vulnerable in this regard, available to be hit with alarming frequency by the kind of opposition that would never have troubled him previously.

More significantly, Ali learned that he could take a punch – and perhaps better than any fighter before or since. It was a realisation that would prove fateful going into the toughest period of his career against some of the best heavyweights the sport has ever produced. None were tougher than Joe Frazier. Coming in low while constantly moving his head to avoid his opponents' punches, and in possession of a left hook that remains one of the best ever, Frazier had the style to beat Ali, who in turn had the style to beat him. The result was a trilogy of fights that rank among the most pitiless and brutal boxing has witnessed. The first was held at Madison Square Garden in March 1971. Dubbed the *Fight of the Century*, it eclipsed the hype surrounding it. The ringside seats were taken up by the nation's celebrities, heralding a fashion that continues to this day, wherein the rich and famous are a regular presence at major fights. At this fight, none other than Frank Sinatra filled the role as the fight's official photographer, while Burt Lancaster was enlisted to help with the television commentary. After a merciless 15 rounds, Frazier won by unanimous decision to hand Ali the first defeat of his professional career. The fight was notable for the vicious left hook Frazier landed in the last round to put Ali on the canvas. Even more notable was the way Ali got back up within seconds of going down.

It would be foolish, not to mention dishonest and a great disservice to his memory and legacy, for anyone to try and beatify Ali as a saint. He wasn't. He was all too human, flawed as well as great, a man who at various points revealed a capacity for vindictiveness that serves to puncture the myth. In this regard, there are some who cite the way he punished the likes of Ernie Terrell and Floyd Patterson for daring to call him Cassius Clay rather than Muhammad Ali as examples of this side of his character. Here, though, I disagree. By refusing to acknowledge and call him by his chosen name of Muhammad Ali, both Terrell and Patterson were guilty of trying to destroy his identity and right to be the man he had chosen to be. Looked at in this light, Ali was arguably within his rights to teach them a lesson. If the punishment he meted out was too harsh, where was the referee? Why didn't he step in to stop it? And what about the respective corners of both fighters? Why didn't they intervene if the punishment was so cruel?

No, when it comes to Terrell and Patterson, Ali could not be accused of cruelty. Boxing by its very nature is a cruel sport, but not so cruel that it cannot be stopped beyond a certain point by the intervention of the referee or trainers.

Ali's treatment of Joe Frazier prior to the *Thrilla in Manila* in 1975 was a different matter. The climactic and most famous fight of the three they fought did reveal an unsavoury side to Ali's character, wherein he mercilessly ridiculed, humiliated and verbally assaulted Frazier. In this, there was none of the tongue-in-cheek humour that usually laced his pre-fight antics. He berated Frazier as an Uncle Tom and at one point produced a toy gorilla as a derogatory representation of his opponent, which he proceeded to punch and taunt in front of the world's press. He also described him as the white man's champion even though Frazier, the son of a sharecropper in South Carolina, hailed from a background that made Ali's appear affluent by comparison.

The irony is that neither man would have achieved the greatness they did without the other. Perhaps Ali's need to humiliate Frazier reflected the extent to which he feared him. For there is no doubt that Smokin' Joe was his toughest opponent, the only man he fought and described afterwards as the closest thing to death he'd ever experienced.

In truth, there are so many epic contests involving Muhammad Ali that it's hard to pick out the greatest. His first fight against Sonny Liston, already mentioned, is up there, as is the Cleveland Williams fight in 1966 in which Ali's movement was so sublime that watching it now still induces awe. Then there's the first and third Frazier fights; the inhuman courage he displayed in his fight against Ken Norton in 1973, ten rounds of which he fought with a broken jaw. The list goes on.

However, no retrospective of Muhammad Ali's career is complete without the *Rumble in the Jungle* in 1974, when the ageing former champion challenged a young, hungry and undefeated George Foreman for his world title. No one gave

Ali a prayer, including members of his own camp. The logic appeared indisputable: Foreman had demolished Frazier and Norton, both of whom had previously defeated Ali. Surely, then, Ali was facing certain defeat against Foreman himself. Worse still, surely he was in danger of being seriously hurt.

Ali had long wanted to fight in Africa – to 'come home', as he put it. In the run-up to the Foreman fight in Zaire, recorded for posterity in the award-winning documentary *When We Were Kings*, he spared no opportunity to bask in the adulation he received everywhere he went in the impoverished African state. Rather ironically, Zaire (now Democratic Republic of Congo) at the time was ruled by one of the most despotic and cruel dictators the developing world had seen in the person of Joseph Mobutu. In 1960, Mobutu toppled and ordered murdered the pan-Africanist leader of the former Belgian colony, Patrice Lumumba, in a CIA-backed coup.

Mobutu was made army chief of staff by the new president, Moise Tshombe, before himself taking over the presidency of the country after organising a second coup in 1965. Thereafter, he ruled the newly created republic of Zaire with an iron fist, wherein torture, murder and the ruthless suppression of dissent prevailed. The dictator regarded and treated the country and its wealth as his personal possession. His motivation in staging the *Rumble in the Jungle*, spending millions of dollars for the privilege even though so many of his people were mired in abject poverty, was to paint his regime in a positive light to a largely disinterested global media. Rather than 'coming home' to Africa, Ali was inadvertently helping to legitimise a ruthless US-backed dictatorship. That said, the champ's motives were unimpeachable, made clear in the aforesaid 1996 Leon Gast documentary of the fight, one of the best, if not very best, sports documentaries made.

Regarding the fight itself, by calling on the deep reserves of self-belief that made him the unique and towering figure he was, Ali unveiled his now-famous rope-a-dope, designed to absorb Foreman's venom on the ropes for the best part of seven rounds before exploding off them in the eighth to knock him out after Foreman had punched himself out. Boxing had never seen anything like it, and it was entirely fitting that it was witnessed by millions around the world watching via live telecast.

Sadly for Ali, though, the only way from there was downhill.

The years of his physical decline mark a tragic bookend to his extraordinary life. The onset of Parkinson's was the steep price he paid for the decades of glory, magic and inspiration he enjoyed and provided to the world. Yet a man who bestrode that world like a Colossus could not in the end defeat his most difficult opponent – namely himself. The result was him going on way past the point of no return. It didn't help that he had many mouths to feed in the form of a large entourage, most of whom took more than they ever gave. His most public appearance in this the third act of his life came at the opening ceremony of the 1996

Olympics in Atlanta, where he was accorded the honour of lighting the Olympic torch. Standing there in the world's gaze, struggling to control his shaking limbs, the circle had closed. From charismatic and precocious boxer to defiant rebel and symbol of pride for a people struggling for equality and dignity, Muhammad Ali finally morphed into a benign figure beloved by the very establishment that once reviled him. His life was the story of a race struggling for respect and justice during one of the most convulsive periods in US history. He was a product of that history. It shaped him and he in turn helped shape it. It was also in Atlanta that he was presented with a gold medal to replace the one he lost after the 1960 Games in Rome. Here, another myth was dispelled, the one that told how he threw his Olympic medal away in disgust upon returning home to Louisville to find himself barred from eating in a whites-only restaurant. He didn't throw the medal away; he lost it.

But, saying that, what did it matter? The legend and the man were by now completely intertwined.

Muhammad Ali lived his life with joy, defiance, courage and poetry. He refused to bow when bowing was the default position of his people and spent his best years defying the odds both in and out of the ring. As he boasted after winning the heavyweight title for the first time against Sonny Liston as a precocious 22-year-old, 'I shook up the world! I shook up the world!'

Yes, Muhammad, you certainly did.

ALI WASN'T the only one who failed to treat Joe Frazier with the respect he deserved. Frazier's home city of Philadelphia – or Philly – was also guilty as charged over the years. Despite Frazier's undoubted achievements in the squared circle, Philly decided to commemorate its vaunted reputation as a boxing hotbed by erecting a statue of Rocky Balboa, the movie character played by Sly Stallone, in what could only be described as a travesty.

When Frazier passed away in November 2011 boxing came together to pay tribute, as befitting a genuine legend of the sport. Yet it was a case of too little too late when we consider that Frazier's later years were spent living above his gym in a less-than-salubrious part of the city he called home. His health and most of his wealth had deserted him – evidence, if any more were needed, that boxing remains stuck in the dark ages when it comes to looking after its own.

Champions, current and former, and various leading lights within the sport took to the airwaves, social media, sports pages and websites to eulogise Smokin' Joe upon his passing, but it begged the question of where were they when he was struggling to make ends meet? Where was their admiration and concern then? Just where is the fund for ex-champions who fall on hard times? Where is the healthcare and pension plan to support the men who carry with them the physical effects of years in the ring giving everything?

It later emerged that Frazier only realised he had cancer when it was too late to be treated. If he had had decent healthcare coverage and the luxury of regular health checks, it probably would have been detected at an early stage and he may have survived. The brutal truth is that Joe Frazier was allowed to wither on the vine, reduced to living above a gym with little to comfort him except memories of bygone days of yore. While he may have made some bad business and financial decisions after he retired from the sport, was this reason to let him end up as he did? The manner of his passing, the poverty and straitened circumstances of his last years, should have been a wake-up call.

The accolades and plaudits champions such as Frazier receive in their prime are all well and good, but it's when their careers end and they are no longer fit for purpose in the ring that the sport's unsavoury character is too often exposed. Frazier was a great champion, but he was also a human being. When he required more than a pat on the back or memories to live on, boxing turned its back on him. More than any other factor, this was the abiding tragedy of his life and passing.

Two years after the death of Frazier, another great from the golden age of seventies heavyweights also passed away.

As with Smokin' Joe, Ken Norton's career was inextricably linked to that of Muhammad Ali. As with Frazier, Norton fought Ali three times: twice in 1973 and again in 1976. A former US Marine, Norton possessed the physique of a Mr Universe and the fighting heart of Rocky Marciano in one scintillating package of heavyweight potency. He won the first in his own trilogy against Ali, taking a 12-round split decision in San Diego. Prior to the fight, Ali entered the ring in a sequin robe presented to him by Elvis. Neither he nor the sportswriters covering the fight envisaged anything other than a comfortable night's work. How wrong they were. Instead, it turned out to be one of the hardest fights of Ali's career and only his second defeat. This particular fight's place in history, however, is secured by virtue of him having fought most of it with a broken jaw. Norton maintained that he broke Ali's jaw in the 11th round, while Angelo Dundee in Ali's corner claimed it happened much earlier. Regardless of when precisely it occurred, it was a loss that succeeded in adding another level to the towering myth of Ali. As for Norton, he never quite gained the respect he deserved as one of the best heavyweights to grace a boxing ring during the division's golden era, fated to be remembered as bridesmaid to Ali's legend.

The rematch took place six months later in Los Angeles. It ended in another split decision, this time in favour of Ali, while the third and final instalment was fought at New York's Yankee Stadium in 1976. Unlike the previous two encounters, the last fight was for the heavyweight title that Ali had won from George Foreman in their epic encounter in Zaire two years earlier. It proved to be one of the most controversial heavyweight fights of the decade, when the champion was awarded a unanimous decision, evidence that the judges must have sat through the bout wearing blindfolds. The crescendo of boos that cascaded from the stands when Ali's hand was raised was the only verdict that carried any credibility that night. Indeed it was one of those nights when boxing adopted the clothes of an impostor, the sporting equivalent of a burglar climbing through a bedroom window in the small hours of the morning to make off with the family silver.

Ali was never able to get to grips with Norton's style and unique cross-arm defence. The heavily muscled Marine possessed a lightning-fast jab, which he threw up from the waist, thus ensuring that his opponents couldn't see it until a split second before it landed. Norton also possessed a left hook that, alongside Frazier's, was considered the best in the business. In an interview a few months after their last fight, Ali was admirably candid in his appraisal of Norton and the bout's unedifying outcome.

'Kenny's style is too difficult for me,' he admitted. 'I can't beat him, and I sure don't want to fight him again. I honestly thought he beat me in Yankee Stadium, but the judges gave it to me, and I'm grateful to them.'

This was an era in boxing when the best fought the best, and often more than once. The only man Norton never met in the ring was Joe Frazier, though they did spar together. Both were trained by the legendary Eddie Futch, which together with the fact they were good friends outside the ring is why they never fought.

In 1978 Norton took part in what many consider to have been one of the greatest fights of all time, against Larry Holmes. Holmes is probably the most under-appreciated heavyweight champion there has ever been, due primarily to his reign at the top coming after the giants of the golden age had left the stage to be replaced by, Holmes excluded, heavyweights of a lesser stamp. His encounter with Norton, in which the latter's WBC title was on the line, was a 15-round war during which Norton hardly took a backward step, repeatedly getting tagged with crushing jabs and right hands as he took the fight to Holmes. In the end, the judges favoured the younger man by split decision – yet another that went against Norton.

Ken Norton was never the same after this fight and should have retired. Instead he fought on, retiring five fights later in 1981 after being stopped in one round by Gerry Cooney. He was deservedly inducted into the World Boxing Hall of Fame in 1989 and the International Boxing Hall of Fame in 1992.

LIVING IN Scotland afforded me the opportunity to follow the career of Ricky Burns up close. Here was a fighter who exemplified dedication, tenacity and courage. Despite not being blessed with an abundance of natural talent, uncommon application and will took him from obscurity, working at a sports shop in his home town of Coatbridge just outside Glasgow, to world titles at two different weights.

The Fighting Scots Gym was housed in what could only be described as a large hut on the fringes of Shotts, a sprawling housing scheme on the eastern outskirts of Glasgow. Under its roof training in the period concerned was, along with Burns, some of the best boxing talent in Scotland – the likes of Craig McEwan, Stephen Simmons, Michael Roberts Jr, and David Brothy. The owner of the Fighting Scots Gym, and trainer of the aforesaid roster of fighters, was Billy Nelson. Nelson was a supremely confident, rumbustious man who'd learned his trade while working with another

Scottish world champion, Scott Harrison, in the role of chief assistant to Harrison's father and trainer, Peter. Nelson had trained Ricky since 2006, taking over after he suffered his first professional defeat against Alex Arthur. Ever since, Ricky had been on a winning streak, culminating in him winning first the WBO super featherweight title, followed immediately by the WBO lightweight title.

Burns was impressively unaffected by the success he'd begun to enjoy in the ring, and with it his regular appearances in the back pages of the Scottish press and wider boxing media. Absent from his make-up was any sign of the bullshit and histrionics that all too often typified the sport. Balancing his achievements in the ring was refreshing-to-see humility and respect towards everyone he came into contact with outside, including his opponents. He was a fighter who seemed to view the promotional aspect of the sport on a par with picking his way through radioactive waste. The product of a working-class upbringing in Coatbridge, Burns came over as a fighter who regarded public acclaim as a source of embarrassment rather than satisfaction or affirmation. Further evidence of his lack of vanity or ego was provided by the fact that even after winning the world title, when money began to fill his bank account after years spent fighting for a pittance, he continued with his part-time Saturday job as a sales assistant at a local sports shop in his home town. Such determination to remain in touch with reality was about as common as hen's teeth when it came to fighters operating at his level.

At the time of writing these words, late 2019, the fact that Ricky Burns is still active, evincing no sign of plans to retire, this is an astonishing feat in itself.

I will never forget the night he entered the ring at the Emirates Arena in Glasgow to face Puerto Rico's Jose Gonzalez in May 2013; he'd been out of action for eight months due to two of his previous fights having been cancelled for one reason or another. It prompted him to leave Frank Warren's promotional stable for pastures new with Eddie Hearn and Matchroom, who with their Sky Sports TV deal had risen to prominence in a blisteringly short space of time. They had hoovered up a who's who of domestic talent to first challenge then supersede Warren's long reign as the nation's premier promoter. Even though Eddie Hearn was a young, smooth and cocky Essex geezer with the features of a *GQ* model, he'd proved he was more than a silver-spooned product of his old man Barry Hearn's success. He'd elevated Matchroom Boxing from an outfit associated with small-town and small-venue shows to being responsible for organising and promoting the biggest fight in post-war British boxing history between Carl Froch and George Groves at Wembley Stadium in 2014.

Returning to Burns, the fact he'd been out for a year meant more pressure, expectation and anticipation than was usual underlay his fight against Gonzalez. I was ringside, covering the fight for a newspaper, and when he started his ring walk you could almost hear the roof crack in response to the wall of noise that greeted him. I studied Gonzalez, who was already in the ring, looking for evidence that the crowd was getting to him. There was none to be had.

Ricky on the other hand appeared flustered as he climbed inbetween the ropes, almost as if the partisan crowd was an unwelcome irritation rather than source of motivation. After just two rounds, it was evident that the time he'd been out had taken its toll, with his timing and sharpness both below par. By the third he'd lapsed into that most dangerous territory of all for a boxer – predictability – resulting in Gonzalez countered his shots with alarming frequency. Ricky, now, was fighting like a man who was over anxious to please the crowd, forcing his shots instead of letting them flow and thus leaving himself exposed. In each succeeding round he was being rocked by the taller Puerto Rican's counterpunches and looked out of ideas. By the seventh I had him way behind and felt sure he was on the way to losing his title.

But then the unbelievable happened. Gonzalez came out in the seventh and launched an all-out assault, akin to that unleashed by the forces of General Zhukov at the gates of Moscow in 1941. The challenger and his corner clearly sensed that Ricky was there for the taking and decided it was time to bring matters to an end. The result was Burns spending most of the round against the ropes being taken apart. Miraculously, he somehow survived and at the bell walked back to his corner like a man who'd just looked into the abyss, cleared his throat and spat in its maw before pulling back.

The eighth saw Ricky dominate proceedings for the first time. The Puerto Rican hadn't recovered from the previous round, in which he'd rolled the dice and emptied his tank in an attempt to get the champion out of there. But he and his corner had miscalculated, with the result that he was now struggling against the resurgent Scotsman, who started to put him on the back foot. Regardless, despite Ricky's dominance continuing on into the ninth, it was too little too late. There just weren't enough rounds left for him to be able to claw back the deficit.

Here, though, is where the incredible took place. Gonzalez refused to come out for the tenth, citing an injured arm. The arena went nuts. Against all logic, not to mention the scorecards, Burns had managed to hold on to his title. It remains a matter of conjecture whether it was an injured arm or broken heart that forced Gonzalez to quit on his stool. The slick Puerto Rican had nothing to be ashamed of if it was the latter. Even Superman would've struggled to overcome the unyielding iron wall of determination in the shape of Ricky Burns that night.

At the post-fight press conference, the room was buzzing as the assembled media waited for Ricky and promoter, Eddie Hearn, to appear. A spontaneous round of applause from the journalists and writers present greeted him when he walked in. Some of those present had covered some of the most dramatic nights in British boxing over many years, yet even they understood that what they'd just witnessed was a demonstration of courage and heart to rank with any that had ever unfolded in a boxing ring.

There was no denying that Ricky had under-performed, though, forced to rely on heart and guts to see him through. And, yes, while there were legitimate reasons for his being under par – the main one his prolonged period of inactivity, which had resulted in ring rust – I couldn't help thinking that at least part of the reason he spent most of the fight being outclassed was simply because he had come up against a higher calibre of opponent than he'd faced up to this point.

I asked him if the crowd had in any way affected his performance, his desire to put on a show after the long absence leading him to try and force things. He denied this had been a factor, citing the length of time he'd been out of action as the reason why he hadn't looked himself.

Ricky's next outing in 2013 came against another transatlantic challenger, this time in the shape of Mexico's Ray Beltran, who trained out of Freddie Roach's Wild Card Gym. Most expected Ricky to overcome Beltran with relative ease given that his opponent didn't have a roster of top names on his record. Beltran, however, had spent the past few years as a regular sparring partner of Manny Pacquiao, which was itself reason not to underestimate him.

The venue this time was the Scottish Exhibition and Conference Centre (SECC) on the edge of Glasgow. As with Ricky's last fight against Jose Gonzalez, the crowd made a strong case for why the most passionate boxing fans anywhere in the world are to be found in Glasgow.

After a good start, which saw the champion establish his signature pumping stiff jab, things began to deteriorate for Burns. By the fourth round Beltran had asserted dominance, walking the Scotsman down and peppering him with body shots and hooks almost at will. The champion's shots in response seemed to be having no effect, Beltran walking through them to force him back on to the ropes round after round. It became hard to watch and when Beltran put Burns down with a vicious right hook in the eighth, it was clear that, unlike in the Gonzalez fight, this time there was no way back.

Summoning up his by now customary reserves of willpower and grit, Ricky held on and survived to the final bell. As soon as it sounded, Beltran and his team immediately started celebrating, knowing as everyone watching knew that the title was on its way back to the States. The revelation that Ricky had suffered a broken jaw quickly spread among us in the press section at ringside. As he stood with Beltran waiting for the judges' decision, you could tell that this was more of a factor in his dispirited body language and demeanour than the likely result. When it was later confirmed that Burns had fought most of the fight with the injury, it would become one of the night's two main talking points. The other – and by far the more controversial – was the judges scoring the fight a draw.

The silence in the arena that greeted the decision told its own story. Words such as 'travesty' aren't sufficient to describe the feelings you experience when you witness such a glaring injustice. Beltran and his team were crushed. Months of preparation, training, diet and focus were instantly rendered futile. The decision was an insult not only to the Mexican-American challenger but also to Burns and to boxing itself. The two-weight world champion would not have enjoyed the embarrassment of having his hand raised as the joint winner of a fight he knew beyond doubt that he'd lost. But then, as mentioned, he had other things on his mind – such as getting to a hospital.

It was a subdued Eddie Hearn who answered questions at the post-fight press conference on this occasion. He was honest enough to admit that Beltran should have got the decision, while claiming, and with a straight face, that the fight may have been closer than people thought. He endured a bit of a hard time from the same press pack that just a few months before had given Ricky a spontaneous round of applause when he appeared in the press room after the Gonzalez fight. Nobody attributed any blame to Ricky Burns for the debacle we'd just witnessed; nor, in truth, did anyone I spoke to attribute any blame to Eddie Hearn. But, regardless, there had been enough bad judging decisions in recent times to warrant a root-and-branch reform of how judges are selected and how they can be made more accountable for their decisions.

Later, driving along a deserted pitch-black motorway on the way home, my emotions were drained. The unbelievable atmosphere that seemed as if it would crack the very walls of the arena was still ringing inside my head. At the same time I was grappling with an unseemly depression over the state of a sport capable of producing nights of such exquisite drama, courage and skill that it reaffirms your belief in the inherent nobility and goodness of the human spirit, but also injustice and cruelty of a type that stews the soul in disgust.

In 2013 British boxing witnessed another even more controversial conclusion to a fight. It came when referee Howard Foster stepped in to stop the action between Carl Froch and George Groves in the ninth round of their clash at the Manchester Arena on 23 November. On this night, Groves put on a performance of such audacity and defiance that he succeeded in turning a crowd that had showered him with boos and jeers during his ring walk into true believers by the end.

All the way through the build-up, Froch had talked like a man who was going to roll over Groves like a juggernaut, rattled it was clear by the younger man's impertinent confidence and self-belief.

Yet it was Groves who appeared the calmer and more focused of the two upon entering the ring, absorbing the chorus of boos in the sold-out arena like a man in possession of a secret weapon about to be unleashed. Froch, the champion, appeared agitated in contrast, and you sensed even before the opening bell that this was going to be a classic.

When Groves declared in the pre-fight press conference that he was going to come out, take the centre of the ring, and engage with the four-time world champion, no one really took him seriously. Most believed his only chance lay in staying on the back foot and utilising his movement to avoid Froch's power, while countering.

But from the opening bell Groves did exactly as promised, beating Froch to the jab while countering with a right that soon began to find the target, forcing the champion back. When Groves put Froch down towards the end of what had been a tempestuous first round with a crushing right hand, a punch Froch walked into with his hands down like a man intent on jumping off a cliff, the fight looked all but over.

Here, though, arrived that element of the human condition that is hard to quantify but is profound in its raw and unvarnished truth. It is measured in the willingness to walk through the door marked 'hell' in order to prevail against seemingly insurmountable odds. Adversity can crush but it can also strengthen. The difference between both remains outwith the ability of science to determine, but in the context of a championship fight in front of thousands of spectators and an army of television cameras, it boils down to the ability to forego the guarantee of a future lived in comfort and health for a precarious present in which you are being asked to risk all in choosing to go out on your shield rather than succumb.

Carl Froch staggered back to his corner at the end of the round on legs that appeared shot. His status and reputation as a warrior had already been cemented when he somehow got up and survived to the bell. The question now was whether he could withstand the inevitable onslaught

Groves was certain to unleash when the bell went at the start of the second. When Froch rose from his stool and ventured out towards the centre of the ring at the start of the next round, his legs looked as if they'd been detached from the rest of his body. He must have known then, as much as he'd ever known anything, that he was about to enter a world of pain.

Groves proceeded to bully and batter him around the ring over the next five rounds. In the midst of the storm, Froch looked like a fighter turning old before our eyes, desperately trying to find a way back into a fight he was losing more with every passing second. In contradistinction, Groves was a fighter transformed, throwing combinations with joyful abandon in the sure knowledge that he was on the verge of making history.

But no amount of conditioning and determination or boxing ability can compensate for the fatigue and psychological deflation that comes with hitting a brick wall for eight rounds without knocking it down. For it was in the eighth that Groves started to tire, just as Froch sucked it up and appeared to catch a second wind. From here it was a ragged affair, both fighters' efforts fuelled by the will and desire that separates champions from contenders when a fight moves into the trenches – that place which no fighter who experiences it ever forgets. No matter, even when Froch had him against the ropes, Groves remained in the fight, countering in between Froch's by now ponderous punches as the fight approached the championship rounds.

By now we all knew that we were bearing witness to an epic.

The crowd's reaction when Howard Foster stepped in to stop the fight in the ninth, after Froch hurt Groves for the first time in the fight, said it all. Foster did what he thought was right, and with just seconds to decide he erred on the side of caution.

But regardless, he had for most watching, and certainly for Froch and Groves themselves, deprived the fight of the definitive ending it deserved.

Froch left the arena as the loser and Groves the champion in the hearts and minds of the crowd in the arena. Such is the cruel and unforgiving nature of the sport that despite waking up on Sunday morning still champion, it's a fair bet that Carl Froch didn't particularly feel like one. He would have been especially hurt by the negative reaction of the crowd to his post-fight interview ringside. For someone as proud and with a deserved reputation as a warrior, the prospect of his legacy being damaged or impaired by a controversial stoppage constituted a gross injustice. Making it doubly unjust was the inarguable fact that when the fight was stopped, he was on top.

Carl Froch deserved better, as did Groves, who fought like a lion only to see his efforts ended by a referee whom most watching the fight believed stepped in prematurely. But Howard Foster is paid to protect fighters from themselves and with that the integrity of a sport that straddles a thin line between nobility and barbarity.

The inevitable rematch came on 31 May 2014 at Wembley Stadium, where a record-breaking 80,000 crowd, and another TV audience of millions, bore witness to the second instalment of what by then had become a domestic rivalry to rank alongside the one shared by Nigel Benn and Chris Eubank in the early nineties.

A left hook-right hand combination in the eighth round of what had been an even contest left George Groves lying slumped against the ropes. It was a single devastating punch that marked an abrupt and worthy conclusion to what had been a fierce rivalry. Froch had entered the ring as the champion and left as the champion. No one now could dispute his rightful status as one of the best fighters Britain has ever produced.

29

I'M SITTING on the ring apron alongside Freddie Roach in the second gym he hadn't long opened downstairs from his main Wild Card gym. Where before the likes of Miguel Cotto and Manny Pacquiao would be forced to prepare for upcoming fights alongside regular members of the Wild Card boxing fraternity, with all the distractions and challenges involved, now they were afforded the ability to work in private.

The last time I'd been here a Laundromat had occupied the space we are sitting in now, as it had between 2000 and 2005 when I lived in Hollywood and trained at Wild Card on a regular basis. Now, today, it's 2015 and we're just three weeks away from the most lucrative fight in boxing history between Floyd Mayweather Jr and Manny Pacquiao, with Freddie having just left me in no doubt about the stakes involved.

'We can't lose this fight,' he said. 'We gotta win this fight. It's for boxing.'

While we're sitting chatting, one of his fighters is working on the heavy bag six feet or so in front of us, and periodically Freddie interrupts our exchange to give him instructions or correct something he's seen in his form that he doesn't like. The fighter in question is Glen Tapia and he's tapering down to the end of his session, after which Manny Pacquiao is due to arrive to start his. When he told me he'd already worked with Miguel Cotto at seven that morning, it was no wonder that he looked weary.

I'd arrived in LA two days previously after a bumpy ride across the Atlantic courtesy of British Airways, scrunched up in economy class adjacent to a guy with a pink Mohican and piercings all over his face who'd boarded the flight drunk and proceeded to annoy everyone sitting in close proximity. We landed at just after seven in the evening local time and I'd arranged to pick up a car at the airport. Anticipating a long wait to get through immigration, I calculated I would reach the hotel some time around ten. Fortunately, unlike my last visit six years ago, when it had taken well over an hour to negotiate immigration, this time there was no queue to speak of and I breezed through. So far so good.

From there, however, my fortunes changed when for some strange reason I had it in my head that you took the 405 South to Hollywood when it's the 405 North. In the shining red VW Beetle I'd opted to rent over the Mercedes and BMW the guy at Avis had offered me as an upgrade, I only realised my mistake after passing signs for Long Beach.

The Hotel Hollywood was located on Cahuenga and Yucca Street, one block north of Hollywood Boulevard. I'd booked the place online after reading some positive reviews, but from past experience you were always a hostage to fortune when it came to budget-priced hotel accommodation in LA. I was therefore hoping for the best while expecting the worst. I arrived at the place just before ten. There was no parking apart from a commercial lot round the corner charging 15 bucks a day. At this hour, and being Scottish and tighter than two coats of paint when it comes to parting with cash, I was reluctant to park in the lot until the next day.

'Fine,' the girl at hotel reception told me, 'you can park at a meter until 8am tomorrow.'

Problem solved.

By now exhausted after the long flight sitting next to the clown with the pink Mohican, I was relieved and delighted to find the room clean with a fridge, cable TV and a large, comfortable bed. Free Wi-Fi ensured I was in clover. I was here for eight nights and as I unpacked the first stirring of excitement arrived at the prospect of returning to Wild Card ten years after I used to be a regular at the place and six years after my last brief visit in 2009. I was especially looking forward to seeing Freddie again, though given that the Mayweather vs Pacquiao fight was almost upon us, I was prepared to be disappointed, knowing how busy he would be.

No matter, I told myself, the worst that can happen is that I enjoy a walk down memory lane and get to experience the madness and energy of a gym I'd long left behind but never forgotten.

At precisely 7.30am the next day, I was up and changed into my running shorts and t-shirt, looking forward to being reacquainted with Runyon Canyon. As the sun streamed in through the blinds on the window, I packed a rucksack with water, clean t-shirt and a piece of fruit, then set off. Down the stairs and out the door of the hotel and along the street I went, soaking up the early-morning heat and sucking in the clean air. I walked round the corner to find an empty space where my car should have been. I was rendered temporarily paralysed while trying to process the disaster that had just arrived. Approaching the parking sign, I read with mounting dismay the warning that cars parked overnight would be towed.

The girl at hotel reception flat-out denied being responsible for having advised me to park there when I faced her up about it.

'You need to read the signs,' she told me.

I went back upstairs to the room and punched the bed umpteen times before getting on the phone to call up the vehicle pound. After confirming that, yes, the car had been towed and it was in their possession, they provided directions and off I went, determined to walk the two miles to the place rather than take a cab and thus wind up even more out of pocket.

So there I was, tramping through Hollywood in the direction of this Hollywood car pound when I should have been enjoying a run through Runyon Canyon. Dressed in running shorts, t-shirt and with a backpack on, I felt like an idiot – and certainly must have looked like one – as I negotiated my way through the local homeless community as it awoke from another night of rough slumber along Hollywood Boulevard.

My misery was only compounded half an hour later when I arrived at the lights at the relevant intersection on Sunset to be met by the sight of the clown with the pink Mohican who'd arrived on the same flight. He was sipping coffee from a paper cup as I joined him, waiting for the light to change. I was so embarrassed I couldn't bring myself to look at him.

Now who's the clown?

A painful $277 later, I retrieved the car and drove up to Runyon Canyon, determined not to allow the experience to crush what morale I had left. I parked on Fuller and set off running. Entering the park was like being reunited with an old friend. The sun was shining and I was back in a part of the world that held a special place, filling me with gladness. The run succeeded in wiping all the shit with the car from my mind, as the memory of the first time I experienced running through Runyon Canyon with Brad 20 years ago returned. I could still remember him telling me as we set off from outside his apartment on Sycamore Avenue just five minutes away, 'You won't make it to the gate.' And I recall vowing to prove him wrong as he sped off, leaving me behind in his vapour trail.

Brad was right, I didn't make it to the gate, having to stop halfway up Fuller with shot lungs. However, over the next three months of my time here back then, I never stopped trying, even though the best I could manage was reaching the top after stopping twice on the way up. I would marvel at Brad, who would run all the way up at a ferocious speed in sweats and with a beanie hat covering his head in the sweltering heat.

Now here I was two decades later, doing the same run comfortably.

Reaching the top, I took my place alongside the bench that had always been there and took in a view of Hollywood and LA beyond. It's a view that fills you with awe, confronted as you are by the monumental size and scale of a city that promises everything but for many delivers up disappointment and despair. Up here the noise of the traffic is reduced to a distant hum as the endorphins swirl around inside, banishing all things negative to leave you feeling reborn.

Marie was Freddie's able and efficient personal assistant, a woman who took no nonsense as she ensured that nobody gained access to the gym whose purpose was to grab a picture, autograph or even just an illicit look at Manny Pacquiao as he prepared for the biggest fight of modern times, and one of the biggest in boxing history.

Back when I was a Wild Card regular Marie wasn't part of the set-up, and back in those days the very thought of

Freddie having his own PA would have been ludicrous. Things were different now, much different, something made clear to me when I popped up to the gym on the second day of my trip to find my path through the small strip mall blocked by security guards, one of them asking me who I was, where I was going, and if my visit been cleared with Marie in advance.

Fortunately, just as I was doing a bad job of explaining myself, she appeared. The security guy called her over and she told him that she recognised me. I'd only met her briefly during my previous visit six years ago, so either she possessed an exemplary memory for faces or was mistaking me for someone else. Whatever it was, I was relieved to be walking up the stairs to the gym.

I had no business being surprised at all the hoopla. It was 2015 and Pacquiao had progressed from the scrawny little kid I first saw shadowboxing in the ring here in 2001 to the status of national hero and icon in the Philippines and international superstar. Add to this the fact that he was preparing for the biggest fight of his career and the security presence was more than justified.

That said, entering the gym, it was as if I'd never been away. Instantly I saw familiar faces from the past, still here, still part of the chaos and energy that had always made the place special. Wee Sammy was one of those I instantly recognised. He'd moved here from Africa way back when he was a prospect and it was reassuring to see that he was still here, working as a trainer with his own roster of clients.

When he saw me standing by the desk, he came over with his hand outstretched.

'My God,' he said, 'where have you been?'

I wasn't here to work out. I'd arrived in my street clothes, still buzzing after my morning run at Runyon Canyon, wishing now I had brought my training gear as the energy swept me up. After spending a minute talking to Sammy, Marie appeared again.

'Freddie's downstairs if you'd like to go down and say hi,' she informed me.

I hadn't asked her to tell Freddie I was here and so it came as a surprise to find myself heading downstairs to see him. Before I went down, she told me, 'Don't be offended, I say this to everyone. Please don't ask him for tickets, pictures or an autograph.'

I wasn't offended, not in the slightest. Her job was to protect Freddie and I respected that.

'I'm not here for that,' I told her. 'Don't worry.'

'How's Pep?' I asked Freddie, as we continued watching Tapia working the bag, peppering it with combinations.

I'd heard his brother had suffered a stroke some time back, which saddened me as I still retained warm memories of him. I could only conceive that the gym was the poorer for his absence.

'Okay,' Freddie said. 'He's doing better.'

We engaged in more talk about the upcoming fight.

'I've been in plenty big fights,' he said, 'but nothing like this.'

It was hard to reconcile the international fame with the guy sitting next to me. He was just as unpretentious and down to earth as he was during our first-ever meeting in the breakfast place on Hollywood Boulevard 20 years ago. In a part of the world where pretension is as common as bad breath in a dentist's chair, this was no mean achievement.

I experienced something else while sitting alongside him on the ring apron. It was a feeling of sadness over which I immediately rebuked myself. Though he was someone who'd immediately recoil at anyone even hinting at sympathy for him over his Parkinson's, I couldn't help feeling sorry for him. Greek tragedies were written with the Freddie Roaches of the world in mind, people whose lives combine great achievement and personal trial in equal measure. The courage and resilience required to succeed as he had while dealing with such a debilitating disease was surely unquantifiable. It was a cross he'd carried for years with dignity and self-possession.

After an hour or so people started turning up, which was my cue to leave. We shook hands, I wished him luck and then left to be smacked in the face by the heat, the memory of our first meeting all those years ago still prominent in my thoughts.

Before heading back to the hotel to freshen up, I needed to grab a bite to eat. Where better than California Chicken on Melrose where Andy, Nick and I used to eat and hang out after training and sparring together? The place hadn't changed a bit. Andy I'd keep in sporadic contact with via the odd phone call, but he was out of town and so I wouldn't be able to catch up with him while I was here. Nick had upped sticks and moved to Phoenix, so I would just have to content myself with memories of those mad sparring sessions and the banter we used to enjoy.

Someone else I was looking forward to seeing was Justin. He was back working with Freddie and Manny, and had been since Manny went down to a brutal KO at the hands of Juan Manuel Marquez at the end of 2012. I was glad to learn they were a team again and so, the following day, I drove over to Fortune Gym a couple of miles east on Sunset Boulevard. I was especially eager to see Justin again having learned from Andy a few months earlier on the phone that he was battling cancer. I'd lost touch with Justin and had been unaware of what he was going through. A quick Google search threw up a couple of YouTube interviews that revealed he was putting a brave face on things. He'd lost a lot of weight and appeared fragile. Knowing Justin as I did, though, he would not be going down without a fight anytime soon.

His gym proved hard to locate. So hard, in fact, that I was forced to rely on the directions provided by a guy standing outside a tattoo parlour on Sunset Boulevard having a smoke. A couple of minutes later and I was walking round the back of the liquor store across the other side of Sunset, accompanied by a warm Santa Ana wind.

Fortune Gym was tucked away behind said liquor store and sitting outside, basking in the late morning sun, was the unmistakeable sight of big Macka. As ever, he had a beanie perched atop his head. As I came closer across the parking lot, he recognised me.

'Hey Scotland,' he called out in his thick Boston accent, 'good to see ya. How you been?'

Justin's wife was behind the desk. She told me that he was on his way and would be arriving soon, so I took the opportunity to have a workout. The place was impressive – spacious, well equipped and clean – with a vibe and an energy that was at odds with the chaos of Wild Card. Two gyms, two contrasting environments, where people pushed themselves in pursuit not only of physical fitness and excellence but, perhaps more importantly, spiritual and psychological nourishment.

'Scottish!' Justin's voice boomed out across the gym, calling me by the name he'd always done.

Not only was it great to see him, it was a relief to note he looked and sounded much improved from the interviews I'd watched before flying over.

We sat outside beside Macka and spent the next hour catching up. When I reminded him of the time we had at the Outlaw Gym in the lead-up to his fight against Lennox Lewis in 1995, a smile came over his face.

'Those were the best times,' he said. 'Boxing was fun then. Now it's full of assholes.'

I moved the conversation on to him and his ongoing battle with cancer. He'd stopped his chemo, he said, as it had been making his life unbearable. Right now his focus was on Manny's fight, after which he was scheduled to return to hospital for tests and to resume his treatment.

Shifting focus to the fight, the conversation got interesting when I asked him if they'd come up with a strategy to deal with Mayweather's defence.

'We've got the gameplan,' he said. 'The gameplan's in place. The question is whether Manny will be able to execute.'

He went on to reveal that much would depend on Manny keeping his lead foot on the outside of Mayweather's lead foot, placing him in position to land his left hand through the middle of Mayweather's guard. Being a southpaw, a left-handed fighter, Pacquiao's ability to manoeuvre Mayweather into position to land with his left while avoiding Mayweather's right coming through the middle of his own guard would prove crucial to the outcome. Such were the technical aspects of a sport that fundamentally amounted to a game of human chess played with fists rather than pieces. Of course, unlike chess, boxing was not a game – especially when it came to a fight upon which so much was riding by way of legacy and history.

Floyd Mayweather's exploits in the ring were up there with all the greats of the past. The extent of his domination of the sport, not only inside the squared circle but also outside, was unparalleled. His ground-breaking deal with US television network Showtime had made him the highest-earning athlete in sport – all of sport, that is. Through his company, Mayweather Promotions, the Michigan-born multiple-weight world champion had commanded hundreds of millions of dollars in pay-per-view revenue over the years, allowing him to enjoy an unprecedented level of control over his career.

In the ring he was undefeated and just two fights away from matching Rocky Marciano's much-vaunted and over-cited record of 49-0. After his previous two fights against Argentina's Marcos Maidana, a consensus had been formed that he'd finally entered the down-escalator of decline. But then again, it was also true that Pacquiao wasn't the same fighter who'd ended the career of Oscar De La Hoya in 2008 and gone on to dominate and stop Miguel Cotto in 2009 either. Yes, he'd bounced back after his crushing KO defeat to Juan Manuel Marquez three years ago with three straight wins against Brandon Rios, Timothy Bradley and Chris Algieri. But none of the aforementioned were Floyd Mayweather Jr's class.

As such, in a very real sense, the result of this fight would largely depend upon who'd deteriorated and declined the least. Freddie had said that the fight was for the soul of boxing. Though some would no doubt dismiss such a sentiment as hyperbole, he was right when we consider the contrast in the way Floyd and Manny conducted themselves away from the ring.

The ostentatious lifestyle of which Mayweather never tired of boasting was a reflection of the society of which he was a product. In fact, so ostentatious was Mayweather's lifestyle that perhaps the only place he experienced reality was inside a boxing ring. As he once said himself, 'Boxing is real easy. Life is much harder.'

Mayweather had, for a number of years, almost single-handedly carried boxing's fortunes on his shoulders as a mainstream sport, rescuing it from the marginal status it had been on the way to lapsing into before he attained such vertiginous heights of fame and notoriety. A Mayweather fight was now a sporting event to rival the NBA, NFL and every other mainstream sport in America. It was his and his fights alone that transcended boxing, lending the sport a legitimacy it had begun to lose for various reasons but mostly due to the inability of promoters and sanctioning bodies to agree a unified approach. Did that make the outrageous money he'd commanded any more justifiable? Not necessarily. But it did prove that boxing still possessed the ability to create excitement and interest. Mayweather's skill in the ring was undeniable. Despite amassing the fortune of a Roman emperor, his hunger and drive remained remarkably undimmed, continuing to maintain a level of application and dedication commonly associated with a broke and hungry novice, rather than a man who'd seen and done it all in the sport over two decades.

As for Manny, his motivation as the fight approached was more selfless. On his shoulders, he carried into the ring the hopes and happiness of a country in which crippling poverty reigned. He was a man who wore his Christian faith on his sleeve and had never forgotten the hardship he'd experienced while growing up in General

Santos City, nor that of those who were back there living in the same destitution now. He knew that every punch he threw was their punch, every victory theirs, allowing them to walk tall, even if only temporarily. It was why he was so revered and lauded by the poor and dispossessed in the Philippines and beyond. To coin an over-used appellation, Manny Pacquiao was a people's champion, not in the same defiant way of a young Ali perhaps but nonetheless a fighter who, as with Ali, stood and fought for something greater than self. This contrast between two men – Floyd Mayweather Jr and Manny Pacquiao – is what made their fight so intriguing, lending it a meaning and significance far in excess of any of their previous fights against other opponents.

It was being labelled the fight of the century – the 21st century, that is – though for me it would be lucky to register in the top ten greatest of all time. Jack Johnson vs Jim Jeffries in 1910; Joe Louis's double header against Max Schmeling in the 1930s; Cassius Clay's first fight against Sonny Liston in 1964, prior to his rebirth as Muhammad Ali; Ali's Frazier trilogy and his *Rumble in the Jungle* against George Foreman; then there were those epic contests involving Hearns, Hagler, Leonard and Duran, known collectively as the Four Horsemen.

No, while Mayweather vs Pacquiao would inarguably prove the most lucrative fight of all time, and the biggest in over a decade, the claim being made by some that it was the greatest ever was simply not credible.

30

EARLY ON the morning of the day of my departure from LA, I stopped by Wild Card for a final workout and to say goodbye to those it had been such a tonic to see again after so many years. I did not expect to see Freddie, anticipating him to be busy downstairs. But just as I finished the workout, he appeared at the counter. I approached, told him I was leaving, and wished him luck.

'Hopefully, we don't need it,' he told me.

Half an hour later, driving down an always-busy 405 freeway towards LAX, I was in a reflective mood. Over the two decades that I'd been around boxing, I'd trained in gyms and attended boxing shows in different towns and cities across the world, rubbing shoulders with fighters ranging in status from novices and amateurs, journeyman professionals, all the way up to world champions and top contenders. What a privilege it had been.

Boxing was one of the last bastions of honesty and authenticity in a dishonest world. Throughout history men have stepped through the ropes to face and triumph over their fears, discovering in the act what it is to be truly alive. There is no lying in a boxing ring, either to yourself or others, making the squared circle as sacred as a place of worship.

Aristotle reminds us that 'The hardest victory is over self.'

Fighters engage in this struggle that the ancient Greek philosopher described on a daily basis in a quest for a kind of transcendence. It is this quest – the kind that can't be measured in titles or money but comes with the very act of stepping through the ropes – that separates those who exist and those who dare to live.

Where to place boxing as a sport in the third decade of the 21st century?

Whenever we take a measure of ourselves in the West, the word civilisation automatically springs to mind. And yet interrupting this smug belief in our own sophistication, up pops a sport like boxing to remind us of the uncomfortable truth that barbarism still has its place. The greatest of them all, Muhammad Ali, said it best, 'Only a man who knows what it is like to be defeated can reach down to the bottom of his soul and come up with the extra ounce of power it takes to win when the match is even.'

Saying that, it would be a mistake to overly romanticise the brutal nature of a sport in which the objective is to punch your opponent in the head more than he punches you, with the intention of rendering him unconscious. I have sat ringside covering fights, watching undercard fighters tear into one another with little finesse or skill and a surplus of bludgeon. In a half-empty arena, without the noise of the crowd to absorb the impact, you are confronted at such moments by the harsh reality of violence for the sake of violence; the sound of punches connecting with skull and torso enough to make you flinch and question yourself for being there.

The vast majority who embark on a career in the pros are fated to go through their careers with nothing much to show for it except an accumulation of bruises and scar tissue. And that's if they're lucky. Slurred speech and an unsteady gait is the too high a price paid by many for the moments of unfettered pride, glory and triumph of spirit they experience.

And yet boxing has endured in one form or another since ancient times, and it will continue to do so long into the future. For no matter what society defines as progress in any given era or age, the excitement, inspiration and ineffable drama of two men facing one another to do fistic battle will always have its place. It is a phenomenon that punctures any amount of talk about humanity having transcended its primordial and primeval origins.

Boxing, ultimately, is not the antithesis of civilisation. It is instead the very essence of it.

In her magisterial work, *Boxing: A Cultural History*, Kasia Boddy asserts that 'At its most cooked, boxing remains raw; at its most bloody, it can still tell a story. Although, as Sonny Liston pointed out, it's always the same story – the good guy versus the bad guy - new versions of good and bad are forever forthcoming. Throughout its long and eventful history as a sport, boxing has remained unfailingly eloquent. At the beginning of the twenty-first century, our appetite for its stories remains undiminished.'

As we move into the second decade of the twenty-first century, who could disagree?

On 2 May 2015, at the MGM Grand Hotel's Grand Garden Arena in Las Vegas, Manny Pacquiao and Floyd 'Money' Mayweather finally met in the centre of a boxing ring. Millions around the world witnessed Mayweather cement his status as the pound-for-pound champion of the world. The occasion proved greater than the actual fight.

Both fighters, since then, have moved on and so has boxing.

Also available at all good book stores

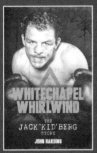

9781785314438

9781785313684

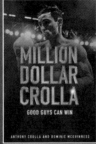

9781785312984

9781785313196

9781785313851

9781785313950

9781785314018

9781785313912

9781785313813